Ernest J. Gaines

WHO WROTE THAT?

LOUISA MAY ALCOTT
JANE AUSTEN
AVI
L. FRANK BAUM
JUDY BLUME, SECOND EDITION
BETSY BYARS
MEG CABOT
BEVERLY CLEARY
ROBERT CORMIER
BRUCE COVILLE
ROALD DAHL
CHARLES DICKENS
ERNEST J. GAINES
THEODOR GEISEL
S.E. HINTON
WILL HOBBS
ANTHONY HOROWITZ
STEPHEN KING
MADELEINE L'ENGLE
GAIL CARSON LEVINE
C.S. LEWIS
LOIS LOWRY
ANN M. MARTIN
STEPHENIE MEYER
L.M. MONTGOMERY
PAT MORA
WALTER DEAN MYERS
ANDRE NORTON
SCOTT O'DELL
BARBARA PARK
KATHERINE PATERSON
GARY PAULSEN
RICHARD PECK
TAMORA PIERCE
DAVID "DAV" PILKEY
EDGAR ALLAN POE
BEATRIX POTTER
PHILIP PULLMAN
MYTHMAKER: THE STORY OF J.K. ROWLING, SECOND EDITION
MAURICE SENDAK
SHEL SILVERSTEIN
GARY SOTO
JERRY SPINELLI
R.L. STINE
EDWARD L. STRATEMEYER
E.B. WHITE
LAURA INGALLS WILDER
LAURENCE YEP
JANE YOLEN

WHO WROTE THAT?

Ernest J. Gaines

Dennis Abrams

Foreword by
Kyle Zimmer

CHELSEA HOUSE PUBLISHERS
An imprint of Infobase Publishing

Ernest J. Gaines

Chelsea House
An imprint of Infobase Publishing
132 West 31st Street
New York, NY 10001

Library of Congress Cataloging-in-Publication Data
Abrams, Dennis, 1960–
Ernest J. Gaines / Dennis Abrams.
p. cm. — (Who wrote that?)
Includes bibliographical references and index.
ISBN 978-1-60413-683-8 (acid-free paper) 1. Gaines, Ernest J., 1933– 2. Authors, American—20th century—Biography—Juvenile literature. 3. African American authors—Biography—Juvenile literature. I. Title. II. Series.
PS3557.A355Z54 2009
813'.54—dc22
[B] 2009022340

Chelsea House books are available at special discounts when purchased in bulk quantities for business, associations, institutions, or sales promotions. Please call our Special Sales Department in New York at (212) 967-8800 or (800) 322-8755.

You can find Chelsea House on the World Wide Web at http://www.chelseahouse.com

Text design by Keith Trego
Cover design by Alicia Post
Composition by EJB Publishing Services
Cover printed by Bang Printing, Brainerd, MN
Book printed and bound by Bang Printing, Brainerd, MN
Date printed: May 2010
Printed in the United States of America

10 9 8 7 6 5 4 3 2 1

This book is printed on acid-free paper.

Table of Contents

FOREWORD BY
KYLE ZIMMER
PRESIDENT, FIRST BOOK

HUMANITY IS POWERED by stories. From our earliest days as thinking beings, we employed every available tool to tell each other stories. We danced, drew pictures on the walls of our caves, spoke, and sang. All of this extraordinary effort was designed to entertain, recount the news of the day, explain natural occurrences—and then gradually to build religious and cultural traditions and establish the common bonds and continuity that eventually formed civilizations. Stories are the most powerful force in the universe; they are the primary element that has distinguished our evolutionary path.

Our love of the story has not diminished with time. Enormous segments of societies are devoted to the art of storytelling. Book sales in the United States alone topped $24 billion in 2006; movie studios spend fortunes to create and promote stories; and the news industry is more pervasive in its presence than ever before.

There is no mystery to our fascination. Great stories are magic. They can introduce us to new cultures, or remind us of the nobility and failures of our own, inspire us to greatness or scare us to death; but above all, stories provide human insight on a level that is unavailable through any other source. In fact, stories connect each of us to the rest of humanity not just in our own time, but also throughout history.

This special magic of books is the greatest treasure that we can hand down from generation to generation. In fact, that spark in a child that comes from books became the motivation for the creation of my organization, First Book, a national literacy program with a simple mission: to provide new books to the most disadvantaged children. At present, First Book has been at work in hundreds of communities for over a decade. Every year children in need receive millions of books through our organization and millions more are provided through dedicated literacy institutions across the United States and around the world. In addition, groups of people dedicate themselves tirelessly to working with children to share reading and stories in every imaginable setting from schools to the streets. Of course, this Herculean effort serves many important goals. Literacy translates to productivity and employability in life and many other valid and even essential elements. But at the heart of this movement are people who love stories, love to read, and want desperately to ensure that no one misses the wonderful possibilities that reading provides.

When thinking about the importance of books, there is an overwhelming urge to cite the literary devotion of great minds. Some have written of the magnitude of the importance of literature. Amy Lowell, an American poet, captured the concept when she said, "Books are more than books. They are the life, the very heart and core of ages past, the reason why men lived and worked and died, the essence and quintessence of their lives." Others have spoken of their personal obsession with books, as in Thomas Jefferson's simple statement: "I live for books." But more compelling, perhaps, is the almost instinctive excitement in children for books and stories.

Throughout my years at First Book, I have heard truly extraordinary stories about the power of books in the lives of children. In one case, a homeless child, who had been bounced from one location to another, later resurfaced—and the only possession that he had fought to keep was the book he was given as part of a First Book distribution months earlier. More recently, I met a child who, upon receiving the book he wanted, flashed a big smile and said, "This is my big chance!" These snapshots reveal the true power of books and stories to give hope and change lives.

As these children grow up and continue to develop their love of reading, they will owe a profound debt to those volunteers who reached out to them—a debt that they may repay by reaching out to spark the next generation of readers. But there is a greater debt owed by all of us—a debt to the storytellers, the authors, who have bound us together, inspired our leaders, fueled our civilizations, and helped us put our children to sleep with their heads full of images and ideas.

WHO WROTE THAT? is a series of books dedicated to introducing us to a few of these incredible individuals. While we have almost always honored stories, we have not uniformly honored storytellers. In fact, some of the most important authors have toiled in complete obscurity throughout their lives or have been openly persecuted for the uncomfortable truths that they have laid before us. When confronted with the magnitude of their written work or perhaps the daily grind of our own, we can forget that writers are people. They struggle through the same daily indignities and dental appointments, and they experience the intense joy and bottomless despair that many of us do. Yet somehow they rise above it all to deliver a powerful thread that connects us all. It is a rare honor to have the opportunity that these books provide to share the lives of these extraordinary people. Enjoy.

A photo of the Conservatory in Golden Gate Park in San Francisco, California. Although Ernest J. Gaines loved San Francisco and often visited this park, he felt he needed to return to his childhood home in Louisiana in order to write his first novel.

1

Going Home

THE YEAR WAS 1962. Ernest J. Gaines, 29 years old, had been living in San Francisco for seven years, first as a student and then as an aspiring writer. Life for him then was a constant struggle: Working a series of part-time office jobs, trying to make ends meet, he was often forced to sneak away from his bosses to write down his ideas and notes on pieces of paper towel and toilet paper in the office bathroom. Times were so hard and money was so scarce that he could not afford a telephone and lived on a cheap and steady diet of pork and beans and hot dogs. It was all he could afford.

Still, he was determined to make it as a writer. There was nothing else that he wanted to do. So he wrote when he could, waking up early to write before work, and then spending late hours alone in his apartment writing until he could not keep his eyes open another minute.

After much struggle, his hard work paid off—he managed to get a couple of short stories published. But there is little pay and virtually no critical notice for short stories written by unknown authors that are published in small, obscure magazines. Gaines knew that if he wanted to be recognized as a writer, he would have to finish the novel he had been working on for several years. Getting that novel published and noticed by reviewers would be an important first step in establishing himself as a writer.

There was one problem, though. Gaines was having an extremely hard time writing his novel. He felt lost, at

Did you know...

While struggling to complete his first novel, Ernest Gaines, like many aspiring writers, lived a hand-to-mouth existence with no extra money for "luxuries." He was so poor, in fact, that one Christmas, he was unable to buy a gift for his mother. He also lost a girlfriend when he could not even afford to buy her a hamburger at McDonald's! One thing that kept him sane, though, was easy (and free) access to San Francisco's Golden Gate Park, which he has described as the "most beautiful urban park in the world."*

* Anne K. Simpson, *A Gathering of Gaines: The Man and the Writer*. Lafayette: The Center for Louisiana Studies, University of Southwestern Louisiana, 1991, p. 29.

odds with himself and his surroundings, and it showed in his struggle to find a voice for his book. Gaines had never been a part of the San Francisco hipster scene, and although he enjoyed living there and had good friends around him, it did not feel like home. And, in fact, it was not home. His true home was somewhere he did not think he really wanted to be.

Ernest J. Gaines had grown up in rural Louisiana at a time when Southern society was racially segregated. In fact, the treatment of African Americans had changed little since the abolition of slavery during the Civil War (1861–1865). As a young African-American boy, he had been forced to work long hours toiling in the fields, and he had arrived in California with just the skimpiest of educations. Although he knew he needed a change in order to complete his book, he was also fairly certain that returning to *that* society was not the change he wanted or needed.

He considered going to Mexico to stay with friends until he finished his novel. But Mexico was not home either. Home was Louisiana, with all its faults and all its strengths. He found himself torn and undecided about what to do, until he read a story in the newspaper about a man named James Meredith. What he read in that story and in follow-up stories changed the direction of the young author's life. But who was James Meredith and why did Gaines find his story so compelling?

JAMES MEREDITH

James Meredith, born on June 25, 1933, was an African American who served his country in the U.S. Air Force for nine years before attending Mississippi's historically black Jackson State College. But Meredith dreamed of attending the University of Mississippi. That school was,

James Meredith, the first black American to graduate from the University of Mississippi, is shown in New York City, on April 27, 1965. Meredith's struggle inspired Ernest J. Gaines to return to Louisiana.

however, an all-white school—blacks were not permitted to enroll.

But on October 1, 1962, Meredith, thanks to the advances made by the civil rights movement that had been growing since the 1950s, became the first black student to attend the University of Mississippi. Showing tremendous grace under pressure, he found himself enrolled at a school where a large number of students hated his very presence. He found himself constantly harassed: When he walked into the cafeteria for meals, the students eating there would turn their backs. If he sat at a table with other students, all of whom were white, the students would move to another table.

Reading about Meredith's struggle to break through the accepted boundaries for blacks in Mississippi, Ernest Gaines found the inspiration he needed: "I kept thinking and thinking about this brave, very brave man—and told myself that if James Meredith can go through all this—not only for himself, but for his race (and that included me as well)—then I, too, should go back to the source that I was trying to write about."[1]

So, despite his worries, on January 3, 1963, Gaines packed up his belongings and returned to Baton Rouge, Louisiana. It would be only his third visit home since he had left for California at the age of 15 in 1948, when he went to live with his mother and her new husband. This time, however, it would not be a quick trip home to visit family and friends. He planned on staying for several months.

Upon arrival, he was immediately reminded of why he had not been eager to return. Once again, Gaines was confronted with the everyday indignities faced by African Americans throughout the South: bus stations and drinking fountains segregated by race, and restaurants reserved for "whites only," where blacks were forced by law to eat separately from whites, sometimes in the basement. After years of living in nonsegregated California, it was a huge shock to his system.

And yet, despite the pain and difficulties it caused him, coming home to Louisiana proved to be just what Gaines needed as a writer. In his essay "Miss Jane and I," he writes:

> I talked to many people, but most of the time I tried listening—not only to what they had to say, but to the way they said it. I visited the plantation that I had tried to write about, while I was in San Francisco. Many of the people whom I had left nearly fifteen years before were still on the plantation. Some were dead, but the ones living could talk about them and did talk about them as though they had simply walked into another room a few minutes before.[2]

He had struggled for years to write about Louisiana while living in San Francisco. But by returning home, listening to the people, and regaining a sense of where he had come from and who he was, Gaines was able to rediscover himself both as a writer and as a man. He later wrote of the experience:

> I do feel deep down in me that the six months I spent in Louisiana definitely saved my writing and quite possibly my life . . . in that I could never have written *Catherine Carmier* if I had not gone South, and maybe I would never have written any other book . . . because my writing is my life. For me not to write is for me not to live. So I went there, put up with many things I hated, but I learned much, much about the people and the place that I wanted to write about. . . . Six months after I left Louisiana the book [*Catherine Carmier*] was finished and it was published about eight months after that.[3]

Ernest J. Gaines, during a visit to his childhood home at the River Lake Plantation in Cherie Quarters, Louisiana, circa 1995.

Although *Catherine Carmier* was not the breakthrough novel he had hoped for, just seven years later, the publication of *The Autobiography of Miss Jane Pittman* changed everything for him. With that masterpiece, Gaines leaped to the forefront of American authors. Returning home had proved to be the key to opening up Gaines's creativity and artistic vision. It made it possible for him to be a writer. Gaines said in an interview in 1976:

> I come back not as an objective observer, but as someone who must come back to write about Louisiana. I must come back to be with the land in different seasons, to travel the land, to go into the fields, to go into the small towns, to go into the bars, to eat the food, to listen to the language. As I said, I don't come back as a scientist, strictly as an observer; I come back to absorb things.[4]

Indeed, throughout his long and illustrious career, Ernest J. Gaines has continued to return "home" to recharge his creativity. All of his books take place within the same carefully delineated geographic territory: the fictitious town of Bayonne, based on the real-life town of New Roads, the closest town to the River Lake Plantation where Gaines grew up.

By keeping his focus on the world he knows so well, Gaines has been able to explore the lives of the people there truthfully, while in the process creating some of the most memorable characters in contemporary American literature. And then, through those characters, his readers are able to learn something new about themselves. As Gaines put it, "My aim in literature is to develop character so that if you pick up the book, you will see something you feel is true, something not seen before, that will develop your character from that day forward."[5]

How did this child of sharecroppers escape a life of grinding poverty and overt racism to become one of America's most respected writers? Why does Louisiana remain his inspiration, and how does he transform life there into art? To discover the roots of his art, we will have to return to Gaines's own plantation childhood in a still-segregated South.

African-Americans workers on a cotton plantation field near White Plains, Greene County, Georgia, in June 1941.

2

Plantation Life

BEFORE THE CIVIL WAR, Louisiana was a state that centered on plantations and slave labor. In 1790, the River Lake Plantation was established by Antoine Decuir, and by the middle of that decade, a plantation house was in place. By 1829, 120 slaves, owned by the Decuir family as surely as were the horses and other livestock, were toiling in the fields and the house. Although slavery was abolished in 1865, many former slaves stayed on at River Lake, working for the family as they always had. While they were free from the whiplash of slavery, many were bound to their former masters financially. All too often, white racist society prevented blacks from seeing themselves as anything but physical laborers, inferior to their white bosses. In many ways, the conditions of their lives had changed little with freedom.

Ernest J. Gaines was born into this world on January 15, 1933, near Oscar, Louisiana, in Pointe Coupee Parish. His home was an old wooden shack, just down the road from the plantation house. Unlike the mansion that the plantation's owners lived in, Gaines's house consisted of just two bare rooms, part of what used to be the slave quarters. It had no running water or electricity. The only source of heat came from the kitchen stove and fireplace.

His mother, Adrienne Gaines, was just 16 years old when her son was born. His father, Manuel, abandoned the family when Ernest was just eight years old, but not before he and Adrienne had had six additional children. To support the

Did you know...

For five generations, members of Ernest Gaines's family had been buried in a graveyard at River Lake Plantation, a cemetery that fell into slow ruin over the years. But no more: Today, Gaines and his wife serve as president and secretary of the Mount Zion River Lake Cemetery Association in Cherie Quarters, Oscar, Louisiana. Funds have been raised to restore the plots, and every year, on the last Saturday of October, Gaines gathers with friends and family to pull weeds, plant flowers, and give the tombs a fresh coat of whitewash, as well as to eat, drink, and remember the past and those who are no longer here.

family, the two had worked as sharecroppers, working in the fields of the same plantation that their ancestors had worked on as slaves 70 years earlier. Indeed, with the exception of being legally free, their lives were no different than those of their grandparents. They were second-class citizens, without any of the rights that we take for granted today.

Growing up in Louisiana in the 1930s and 1940s, Ernest Gaines knew from an early age that discrimination was going to be a central fact of his life. In a 1982 interview, he recalled:

> We were trained to understand these things. Blacks could not afford to forget. I had pressure on me to know and to remember.
>
> I felt the discrimination that any black Southern child would feel. . . . I couldn't eat or drink in certain places. I had to ride the back of the bus and I couldn't go to the bathroom in certain places. I've been hurt and insulted and I've seen the same things happen to my mother, sisters and brothers.[1]

The family was desperately poor. After her husband deserted her, Adrienne Gaines left the plantation to go to New Orleans in search of work. Ernest himself was forced to work in the fields, earning just 50 cents a day. It was a difficult way for the bright, sensitive Gaines to grow up, with the pressures of having to help support his family. He recalled how "it was hard and tough being the oldest child. I had to go into the swamps to cut wood for the stove as well as fireplace. When you're a twelve year old kid trying to pull a saw for half a day, it's about the most cruel thing you can do to somebody."[2]

Yet, looking back, Gaines is able to see the positive side of his childhood as well, noting that he "came from a place where people sat around and chewed sugar-cane and

Ernest J. Gaines is photographed near Cherie Quarters, his childhood home near the False River in Louisiana, circa 1995.

roasted sweet potatoes and peanuts in the ashes and sat on ditch banks and told tales and sat on porches and went into the swamps and went into the fields—that's where I came from."[3]

AUNT TEEN

With his mother working in New Orleans, it fell to his great aunt, Augusteen Jefferson (Adrienne's father's sister, known affectionately as Aunt Teen or Miss Augusteen), to raise Ernest and his brothers and sisters. It is this extraordinary woman who had the greatest influence on Ernest and who showed him the way to survive his difficult childhood. She was, as Gaines described her, "the greatest person, the strongest person I ever knew."[4]

For reasons that were never determined, Miss Augusteen was paralyzed from the waist down at a very early age. She did not let this stop her, though, and spent her life crawling wherever she needed to go, which gave her tremendous upper body strength. She did the work of many, with a sense of pride and determination that would put most able-bodied people to shame. Ernest lovingly remembered her in a 1973 interview with Forrest Ingram and Barbara Steinberg:

> Until I was fifteen years old, a lady raised me who never walked a day in her life. She crawled over the floor as a six month old child might do. She had the strongest pair of arms. She could whip hard. I had to cut and break the switch, bring it to her, kneel down, and get my whipping. She cooked for us. In winter, she sat on a little bench beside the wood stove, where they cut the wood. "Bring the wood there, light the fire," she would say. And she would lean over her little bench and put the wood into this little stove. She could wash. She'd sit on this bench and lean over. We had these old wash boards—you know those old wash boards?—and she'd just

> wash, wash, wash, with an old bar of soap. There was no washing powder then. And our clothes: she also patched our clothes, sewed our clothes, she baked cakes and this sort of thing. But that was not even enough for her. She would, in the evening, when work was done, when she'd cook food and all that sort of thing, she'd crawl over the floor, over the porch out into the garden to work.[5]

Miss Augusteen also encouraged young Ernest, a noticeably intelligent child, to go to school. Of course, the education he received was in no way equal to that of the children going to the white schools. For Ernest, school lasted only from October until April. The rest of the time Ernest, like the children of many sharecroppers, was forced to work in the fields, either planting or harvesting the year's crops.

School was held in the church built on the plantation for the black sharecroppers. There was no electricity. There was no inside toilet, and drinking water was drawn from a nearby well. There were not even chairs or desks; the students were forced to use the pews and benches intended for church services. To write his lessons, Gaines either had to balance his paper and books on his lap or get down on his knees and use the pew as a table. (This scene is revisited in his novel *A Lesson Before Dying*.) Not surprisingly, the quality of the education that Gaines received was sketchy at best, as one underpaid, underqualified black teacher after another attempted to teach too many students without proper books or equipment.

There were, however, other ways for Gaines to learn and gain insight about the world around him. Because his aunt was much beloved in the community and was unable to travel far, her cabin became the center of the plantation's social life once the long day's work ended. Gaines, already a writer without knowing it, spent long hours sitting on his aunt's porch, listening to the stories being told and, without consciously realizing it, filing them away for later use. He described such evenings in a 1971 speech at Southern University in Baton Rouge:

> Then there were the people who used to come to our house, because she [Augusteen] was crippled and could not go to theirs. In summer they would sit on the porch, the gallery—"the garry," we called it—and they would talk for hours. Sometimes there would be only one other person besides my aunt; other times maybe a half dozen. Sometimes they would sew on quilts and mattresses while they talked; other times they would shell pecans and beans while they talked. Other times they would sit there smoking pipes, chewing pompee and drinking coffee while they talked. I, being the oldest child, was made to stay close by and serve them coffee or water or whatever else they needed. In winter they moved off the porch and sat beside the fireplace and drank coffee—and sometimes a little homemade brew—while they talked. But regardless of what time of year it was, under whatever conditions, they would find something to talk about. I would try to put some of this talk in a book which I would title *The Autobiography of Miss Jane Pittman*.[6]

LETTER WRITING

Evidently, there are times when an author does not have to go out looking for material; the material comes to the writer.

By the time Gaines had finished third grade, he was better educated than most of the adults on the plantation would ever be. It would fall to him to help them communicate with the world outside of the plantation, a world that most of them would never know. He recalled:

> I wrote letters for the old people and I read the letters they received, and I read the Bible and the comic strips, and I ordered from Sears Roebuck and Montgomery Ward catalogues for them. But I remember most writing their letters for them. They could never get it down right. Letter-right, I mean. They would talk and talk but it would not be the way you put it down on a letter. That is another thing about the writer—he must be a form-a-lizer. He must be able to put it down right, readable. He must be able to sift through, catch the essence. It would've been better, I'm sure, if the old people could just talk to one another and not have to worry about letter writing, depending on somebody like me. But that was impossible. . . . Someone had to write for them. I was paid nickels and dimes and tea cakes.[7]

Although the pay was small, the lessons that young Ernest Gaines learned from writing letters for those who could not was invaluable. He learned how to take the spoken speech of the people around him, condense it, "form-a-lize" it, and turn it into words on paper. He was learning to turn experience into art.

He was also beginning to express himself through his writing. Not content with just writing other people's letters, he started writing miniplays, some of which were presented at the Baptist church where he had been baptized when he was 12. The plays were humorous mock weddings, with his brothers and sisters as actors. Gaines discussed his early writing efforts with an interviewer for the *New Orleans Review* in 1973:

> I can go back to when I was 13 or 14, and remember that I put on small plays and all. I put them on in this church, and I had to rewrite everything. Not only did I have to rewrite, but I had to be the director. I had something like a little mock-wedding going on. My back was towards the audience and the people who were getting married—and the best men and all—faced the audience. I had my script over the Bible and I would read my part, because I never learned the damned part. So that's the way I started trying to write from the time I was about 13 years old.[8]

Imagine yourself living in the segregated society that Gaines did, surrounded by friends and family who had had few educational opportunities, who were never encouraged to use their minds and create, and still feeling within yourself the overwhelming desire to dream and write and create. It is this need to create that is an essential part of any artist.

ST. AUGUSTINE

Not only was Gaines taking the first small steps necessary to becoming a writer, but he also gained the opportunity to improve his education. In 1945, he began attending St. Augustine, a black Catholic school in the nearby town of New Roads. No buses were provided to transport the black students to the school, so Gaines was forced either to take the local bus or to hitchhike to St. Augustine. Occasionally, the owner of River Lake Plantation, who was also the parish sheriff, would give him a ride to school. Gaines offered to polish his shoes to repay him but was told by the kindly gentleman, who evidently saw something special in Gaines, that he would not have to shine anyone's shoes to make a living.

But after three years at St. Augustine, Gaines had reached the end of the line in terms of getting an education in Pointe Coupee Parish. There was no high school for blacks, and, as appalling as it seems today, blacks were not even allowed to enter the area's public library. To the white government and society, educating African Americans was not only unnecessary but possibly dangerous: An educated person could become someone who would stand up for his or her rights and challenge the segregated society that had endured for hundreds of years.

Gaines himself knew that his chances of becoming more than just another worker in the fields were nonexistent as long as he remained at the plantation. Years later, he said in an interview:

> I'm pretty sure the talent I had was average. I knew kids who were athletic, who would have been great baseball players or fighters or actors or maybe writers or stand-up comedians, or singers. They never got a chance living in a place like that. . . . I hope it [the hard life] never happens again to anyone. Even when I was growing up there I never thought it was the worst sort of life because everybody else around me was the same way. Everybody was poor, wore the same clothes, ate the same food, went to school five months, did the same work. That was life. But the older people always thought it was something else and wanted me to do other things.[9]

Fortunately for Gaines, a change was about to occur that would lift him from the segregated world of Pointe Coupee Parish and into a new life that he could have imagined only in his wildest dreams, one that would open a new world for him.

As a teenager perusing the stacks of the Vallejo Public Library, Ernest J. Gaines grew to love Russian literature. One of his favorite authors is the great Russian novelist and playwright Ivan Turgenev (1818–1883).

3

A New Start

WHILE WORKING IN New Orleans, Gaines's mother, Adrienne, had met and fallen in love with a merchant seaman named Ralph Colar. In 1947, the couple moved to Vallejo, California, just north of San Francisco. Adrienne went to work in a factory, trying to save up enough money to bring her children to Vallejo. In 1948, she sent for her oldest son to come live with her and his new stepfather.

Ernest Gaines was just 15 when he left the rural plantation life he had always known for the nonsegregated world of California. Although he was nervous about the move, deep down he knew it was time to go. Years later, he remarked on the fortunate timing of his move:

> Had I left five years earlier, I would have not have had enough experiences. Had I stayed five years longer, I would have been broken—in prison, dead, insane. . . . I left at the very best time to leave. I knew the quarter and the plantation and the small town. I knew the Catholics, the Baptists, the Creoles, the mulattoes, the problems between black and white.[1]

He had absorbed the experience he would use later in his books. It was time for him to go elsewhere and learn how to use those experiences.

SAYING GOODBYE

It was a Sunday when Gaines left the plantation, his few belongings packed up in a battered suitcase, along with the fried chicken, tea cakes, and pralines that had been prepared for him to eat on his journey. After saying goodbye to the friends and family he had grown up with, he saved his final farewell for his beloved Aunt Augusteen:

> She sat on the floor—just inside the door. "I'm going, Aunty," I said. I did not lean over to kiss her—though I loved her more than I have loved anyone else in my life. I did not take her hand, as I had taken the other people's hands, because that would have been the most inappropriate thing in the world to do. I simply said, "I'm going, Aunty." She looked up at me from the floor. I saw the tears in her eyes. She nodded her head, and looked down again. When I came out into the road, I looked back at her. I waved and smiled; she waved back. The old people were silent all this time—but I'm sure that before I reached the highway to catch the bus they were talking again.[2]

Ernest Gaines, carrying a single suitcase, walked out to the main road to flag down a Trailways bus going to New Orleans. From there, he would take the train to Crockett, California, just across the bay from Vallejo, where his new life would be waiting for him.

THE DOORS OPEN

It was a world unlike any Gaines had ever known. His mother and stepfather were living temporarily in a government housing project. There, for the first time in his life, he found himself surrounded by people of very different ethnic backgrounds: Mexican, Japanese, Chinese, and Filipino. It was an eye-opening life lesson for him, one that demonstrated to him something he had always secretly thought: The world was made up of many groups and types, all equal, trying to work hard and make sense of their lives.

Gaines quickly adapted to his new life, but it was not always easy. In a speech given at Southern University in 1971, he noted:

> I made friends quite easily, and most of the time, especially during the day, I was very happy. But at night when the new friends had gone, I sat alone in a room and thought about home. Many times I wished that my aunt would write my mother and tell her to send me back. Or that some wise man would come up and tell me how futile an education was when I had to sacrifice so much for it.[3]

Soon, Gaines had to adapt to another move. The family moved from the government housing project to an apartment in downtown Vallejo. There, he gave in to the temptation of hanging out in the streets with a "rough" new group of friends. But his stepfather, a strict but loving man, would have none of that. He urged Gaines to get off the street and take advantage of the opportunity that was being given to him to get an education and make something of himself.

At first, Gaines tried to fill in some of his lonely hours by boxing at the local YMCA. But after a short time, he decided to find an alternative. So instead of the world of boxing, Gaines, lonely and homesick for Louisiana, began a solitary exploration of a world he knew nothing about: the world of books and literature.

THE VALLEJO PUBLIC LIBRARY

At age 16, Ernest J. Gaines walked through the doors of a public library for the first time. In Louisiana, public libraries had been for whites only. Can you imagine what he must have felt this first time in the Vallejo Public Library? Seeing all those rows of books, written by authors he knew nothing about, must have been thrilling and terrifying at the same time. What to choose? What to read? Where to start?

He began slowly, just picking a book at random off the shelf, sometimes drawn to nothing more than its cover, reading a few paragraphs or pages, then putting it back. As he grew more confident, he began to explore the fiction section in earnest, but, as he said often in interviews, he did not know what to read, so at first he read anything. He then began searching the fiction section in depth, trying to find books that related to his experience in rural Louisiana, stories that spoke to him as a young African American.

At that time, however, there were no books available either by or about blacks. And the Southern literature that was available, written by whites, presented him with one stereotypical black character after another, far from the very real and human people he knew so well. In his essay "Miss Jane and I," Gaines discussed this experience:

> I found most of the work that I read untrue and unreal to my own experience, yet because I hungered for some kind of connection between myself and the South, I read them anyhow. But I did not care for the language of this writing. I found it too oratorical, and the dialects, especially those of blacks, quite untrue. . . . I did not care for the way black characters were drawn.[4]

There were some things, however, that Gaines thought the Southern writers got right.

> Sometimes they accurately captured sounds that I knew well: a dog barking in the heat of hunting, a train moving in the distance, a worker calling to another across the road or field. . . . These writers, who so poorly described blacks, did well with the odor of grass and trees after a summer rain; they were especially adept at describing the sweat odor in the clothes of men coming in from the fields; you could see, better than if you were actually there, the red dust in Georgia or the black mud of Mississippi.[5]

Once Gaines had read all the Southern writers he could find, he began moving through the best that literature had to offer, regardless of region. He started with John Steinbeck, who wrote so eloquently about the workers in California's Salinas Valley, and Willa Cather, one of America's greatest writers, who wrote beautifully about the land and people of Nebraska.

The more he read, the more he wanted to read. He read the short stories of Guy de Maupassant. He then discovered Russian literature, starting with the short stories of Anton Chekhov, then moving on to the works of Leo Tolstoy,

Aleksandr Pushkin, and Nikolay Gogol, before finally reading Ivan Turgenev, whose *A Sportsman's Sketches* and *Fathers and Sons* would have an enormous influence on Gaines as a writer.

Perhaps somewhat surprisingly, the young man from rural Louisiana found himself strongly drawn to the writers of nineteenth-century Russia. These authors remain among his favorite writers. What connection could a teenage Ernest Gaines possibly feel with writers describing a society and world so different than Gaines had ever known? To this questions, he once answered:

> I felt that they wrote truly about peasantry, or, put another way, truer than any other group of writers of any other country. Their peasants were not caricatures or clowns. They did not make fun of them. They were people—they were good, they were bad. They could be as brutal as any man, they could be as kind.[6]

These Russian writers were able to connect with Gaines because they wrote truthfully about the peasantry of their country. Gaines, who growing up had known so well the poor workers—the "peasantry"—of rural Louisiana, grew to love the Russian authors because of how well they understood the peasants of their own country.

Despite his discovery of Russian literature, he was still dissatisfied. Failing to find works of Southern literature that spoke to his experience, he did what thousands of other writers have done before him: He decided he would have to write them himself. At the age of 16, Ernest J. Gaines knew with blinding certainty that he was going to be a writer:

> I read and read, but I did not see myself and my friends and family and relatives in the stuff that I did read. I didn't see us

in the Southern writers. I didn't even see myself in the Russian writers, although the Russians came close. So I began to try and do it myself and of course, I went back to my childhood to

Did you know...

It is interesting to note that while Russian writers, French writers, and white American authors such as Ernest Hemingway and William Faulkner have heavily influenced Gaines, he says that black writers have had virtually no influence on him. Why is that?

The major African-American novels, notably Richard Wright's *Native Son* and *Black Boy* and Ralph Ellison's *Invisible Man*, were published in the late 1940s and early 1950s. Although these books were published while Gaines was studying literature in school, they were not yet part of the curriculum; it would not be until the 1960s that such novels would be commonly taught in school. So by the time that Gaines had the time to read them, he was already a writer with his own distinctive style. At any rate, the direction that Wright and Ellison went in as writers was not the direction he wanted to go.

There are, however, two exceptions. Gaines acknowledges that Zora Neale Hurston, best known for her masterpiece *Their Eyes Were Watching God*, was an influence on him as a writer. He also insists that if he had read Jean Toomer's novel *Cane* before he had found his own way as a writer, it would have influenced him as well. He says of *Cane* "to *me*, that's the Black American novel. That *is* my novel."*

* John Lowe, ed., *Conversations with Ernest Gaines*. Jackson: University Press of Mississippi, 1995, p. 134.

> write about. I suppose that most writers, when they first start out try to write about their childhood, and this is what I did.[7]

FIRST ATTEMPT

Unable to find in the library the novel he wanted to read, the young man who had just begun discovering literature sat down to write a novel of his own. He went immediately to work, writing 12 to 15 hours a day by hand on yellow typing paper. Then, when he was satisfied with his draft, he slowly—using just two fingers—typed out his manuscript on a typewriter he begged his mother to rent for him.

The book was a love story centering on the children of two African-American families, one light skinned and one dark, separated geographically by a stream. Gaines knew nothing about how to get his book published. The only books he had ever seen were the printed and bound books he had seen in the library. So he cut the pages of his typed manuscript down to what he saw as "book size," wrapped up the package, tied it up with a piece of string, and sent it off to a New York publishing company, certain that it would be published. As Anne Simpson recounts in her study of Gaines, he has often told interviewers the story of the result of his first attempt at entering the world of publishing:

> I thought you just sent it [a manuscript] to them and they put it between covers and it was a book. It came back in that same old string, too. I figure they must have shaken and smelled it and been afraid to try. When they found that it was not food, they probably played football with it a couple of weeks, then decided to send it back to me.[8]

Looking back, Gaines knows that, at age 16 and still catching up on his education, his first book was not good.

"It was possibly the worst novel, the worst number of pages that anyone could possibly call a novel."[9] At the time, though, it seemed to him to be a crushing defeat. He had already imagined how he would spend the money from his book, purchasing his family a new house and a new car, with enough money to spare to send to his younger brothers and sisters still living in Louisiana.

Instead, Gaines took the manuscript and burned it, page by page, in the incinerator. But he was not ready to give up his dream of becoming a writer. He talked his mother into buying him his own manual typewriter. On it he continued to plug away at his writing, using the two-finger typing system he had mastered. As he said in an interview, "I was let down, but I was determined to go on. I had only lost the first battle, not the war—at least not yet."[10] Little did he know how long the war would last or that, years later, his first attempt at writing, "A Little Stream," would be reborn from the ashes of the incinerator to serve as the basis of his first published novel.

GRADUATING, THE ARMY, AND BACK TO SCHOOL

After graduating from high school in 1951, Gaines enrolled at Vallejo Junior College, which was then free to residents. He was the first male in his family to enter college. At Vallejo Junior College, Gaines not only studied hard, but he also participated in track, setting a record for the 220-yard (201-meter) dash that stood for 20 years. Unfortunately, he also badly injured his knee, which has given him trouble since that time and has kept him from participating in any strenuous sports activities.

In 1953, after Gaines graduated from Vallejo Junior College with an associate of arts degree in journalism, he was drafted into the U.S. Army and served for two years in

Guam. While there, he spent more time playing pool and cards than he did writing, but he still managed to win prizes for his short stories in an Army competition sponsored by the U.S. Far East Command in Japan. He received two checks for his efforts, one for $15 and the other for $10. It was the first time that he received any financial reward for his writing. He later said:

> I cashed the ten dollar check but the fifteen dollar check is at the house in a little glass bank that belonged to my aunt (Augusteen) who died on that Louisiana plantation in 1952. After her death, the little glass bank with a few coins were given to me to remember her by. I put the check in the bank when I was discharged from the Army in 1955, and it's been there ever since, because in order to get it out I would have to break the bank open, and that I'll never do.[11]

After serving his time in the military, Gaines enrolled at San Francisco State College, taking full advantage of the $110 monthly payment offered to him by the G.I. Bill to use for his education. (Among other provisions, the G.I. Bill offered returning servicemen loans to help them receive educations, start businesses, or buy homes.) Since it was not enough money to live on, he supplemented his income by working in a post office and for a printer. The majority of his time was spent in the classroom.

Upon entering San Francisco State, Gaines had the discussion that most new students have with their college adviser about their career plans and what courses they should take. He recalled:

> [I] told my advisor that I wanted to be a writer, he asked me what else I wanted to do. I told him nothing else. He broke down the percentage of those people who made a living

> writing—and it was frightening. My being black, he said, the chances of making a living writing would be much harder. I told him I didn't care how hard it would be, I couldn't think of anything else I wanted to do.[12]

Seeing Gaines's determination, his adviser gave up trying to persuade him to find a different career. There was one problem, though. The school did not offer a degree in writing, and for Gaines to get money from the G.I. Bill, he had to work toward a degree. He decided on English as his major and social sciences as his minor. It turned out to be an excellent decision.

By majoring in English, Gaines was able to get the best possible education for an aspiring writer: reading the best that world literature had to offer and studying under professors who were able to show how highly respected authors constructed their works. His professors knew he wanted to be a writer, but they realized that he did not yet have the technical skills necessary for him to write the stories and novels he wanted. To do so, he would need to learn from the masters. Gaines recalls:

> My instructors at San Francisco State . . . thought I would say it all one day—but it would take time. "It will take time and work, time and work," they said, "and read it carefully. Do you see how Turgenev handles this same kind of situation? Bazarov's relationship to his old people in *Fathers and Sons* is the same as what you're trying to do to Jackson and Aunt Charlotte. Now, take Joyce—see how he handles Stephen and his discussion with the priest. Sherwood Anderson—how he handles his people of Winesburg, Ohio. Faulkner—and his Yoknapatawpha County. Read, read, read it carefully. You'll get it. But it will take time—time and work. Much work."[13]

Today, Gaines gives the same advice to any of his students who are aspiring writers: Read, read, read. Write, write, write.

LEARNING TO WRITE

Gaines did not spend all his time at San Francisco State reading the classics. He wrote as well, taking creative writing classes to learn how to apply to his own writing what he was learning from reading the writing of others. His instructors noted Gaines's talent early on. Gaines said they "took an interest in me very early. They singled me out and gave me a lot of help. I was the only black in class. There must have been about twenty to twenty-five people, and I was the only black. They were very encouraging."[14]

He did have problems initially. He struggled in his expository writing class, taught by Stanley Anderson, because writing formal essays was something he still felt uncomfortable doing. He persuaded Anderson to let him write a short story instead of an essay for one particular assignment. The story, "The Turtles," impressed Anderson, who encouraged Gaines to continue writing stories. Several of them were published in the college literary magazine, *Transfer*. Approaching graduation, Gaines included two of his stories, "The Turtles" and "Boy in the Double-Breasted Suit," in his application for a creative writing fellowship to Stanford University.

After receiving his bachelor of arts degree in 1957, Gaines received the Wallace Stegner Creative Writing Fellowship at Stanford. Wallace Stegner, a noted writer and teacher who had founded Stanford's creative writing program, had a nose for talent: Among his students over the years were literary stars such as Ken Kesey, Larry McMurtry, Robert Stone, and Tillie Olsen. Gaines was in elite company.

While important in giving Gaines time to write and study, the fellowship money was still not enough to keep him from having to work a series of odd jobs to help make ends meet. Still, he was more determined than ever to become a writer. He gave himself a goal. In 10 years, he told himself, he would become a successful published writer or he would find a new career. It would be a difficult goal to reach, but Gaines was certain that he could do it.

Ernest J. Gaines sits in the church where he attended school as a boy in Oscar, Louisana. "I wrote plays in this church," he says.

4

Trying to Get Recognized

HE ALMOST DID not make it. His yearlong fellowship was just that, a year in which he was "paid" to take writing classes. And while he appreciated everything he learned, he also came to understand that no one can truly teach you to write. What the fellowship gave him was the opportunity and freedom to do the work that he wanted and needed to do. He said later:

> They didn't teach me how to write. No one does that. It just helps to have people who are in the same thing to talk to occasionally. It seems to me there is only one thing to do about writing: dig into it. You've got to get in a little room with a desk by yourself and do it. You know? Do it.[1]

After the fellowship ended, Gaines found himself working a series of jobs just to be able to afford food and a small apartment. But he still found time to write. While working as a mail clerk for an insurance company, he wrote a first draft of his short story "A Long Day in November" on paper towels in the company's men's room. In less than three weeks, he had written a draft on 250 sheets of paper towels, much to the dismay of his boss. Gaines recalled: "I used to sneak into the bathroom and write on paper towels. My boss would kick the door and yell, 'Get back to work!' and I'd say, 'Don't you know there's a genius at work in here?' "[2]

DOROTHEA OPPENHEIMER

Although making a living was difficult, Gaines did have one advantage that many other aspiring writers do not have—someone in his corner who was convinced of his talent. In 1959, he signed on with a literary agent, Dorothea Oppenheimer, who had been successful at a prominent literary agency in New York City before moving to the West Coast in 1955 to work on her own. Oppenheimer had read Gaines's short story "The Turtles" in *Transfer* and liked it enough to contact some of his instructors at San Francisco State to get their opinions on the young writer's talent and potential.

Based on what she heard, Oppenheimer contacted Gaines himself, telling him she would like to see his work from then on. Until her death in 1987, she remained his agent, his sounding board, his friend. She gave him the confidence he needed to work even when he was unsure that anybody would ever want to read anything he wrote. She made it possible for him to become an author. Gaines recalled that "from then on, everything I wrote in college and after, she saw it. When I got out of school, I had no money at all and she was a patron. She put up money. She was much more than just an agent. As I said, she was patron, friend. She was also editor and secretary."[3]

She told him that as long as he continued to write, she would be there with him. He recalled:

> The first ten years after I got out of college, between '57 and '67, were lean years . . . it was she who stuck by me and paid the rent and cooked food and all kinds of things. So she was much more than just an agent. There'll never be another person like that in my life. I know that. And I'm not in the position I was at that time, because I'm not this beginner who needs this encouragement and someone to stand beside you when everything is falling apart and you don't have anyone else in the world to turn to. She was there. I needed a person like that at the time.[4]

GOING BACK TO THE BEGINNING

At this point in his career, Gaines had achieved his only success with his short stories, a form with which he felt particularly comfortable. But one day in one of his writing classes at Stanford, a visiting editor from New York told him that, while his stories were good, there was no money to be made in writing them. Novels were where the money was. Determined to be a successful writer and knowing he would be broke after leaving Stanford, Gaines decided he should start work on a novel. But what would he write about?

He decided to go back to the beginning, to the novel that he had thrown into the incinerator some 10 years earlier. Believing he had learned a lot about literature and writing in the meantime, Gaines was determined to get it right this time, to put the lessons he had learned in class to good use and write a novel of which he could be proud.

In January 1959, Gaines set to work rewriting "A Little Stream." Later that spring, he received the Joseph Henry Jackson Award from the San Francisco Foundation, which is given to young writers of a complete or work-in-progress manuscript. And while it must have been encouraging for Gaines to be recognized for what he had accomplished on his novel so far, he soon found himself running into one literary roadblock after another. He recalled:

> After winning this award I felt that the rest of the book should be easy and that I should finishing it later that same year. How wrong I was. It turned out that only the first quarter of the book was easy; everything else that followed was but one obstacle after another. My plot was unreal, the dialogue was untrue, and action that I was imposing on my characters was forced. The people and the place were cardboard figures. So everything I wrote one day, I destroyed the next day. Wrote and destroyed, wrote and destroyed.[5]

Despite the difficulties, he kept working. He settled into a work pattern that holds to this day. He would get up at 6:30 or 7:00 in the morning, eat a scanty breakfast, go for a walk, go back to his apartment, settle himself at his desk, and write, working at least five hours a day, five days a week—filling the time in between with whatever part-time jobs he had managed to find.

He worked on the book for four years without completion. To give himself a sense of accomplishment, he also completed two short stories during this period, "Just Like a Tree" in 1962 and "The Sky Is Gray" in 1963. But finishing his novel was his goal. Oppenheimer had already found a publisher for the book, who had paid an advance of $1,500 before seeing the final manuscript. The pressure was on Gaines to finish the book as quickly as possible.

But he found it impossible to get done what he need to in San Francisco. His book was set in the Louisiana he had grown up in, and after years in California, that felt remote and far away. So, as we learned in Chapter 1, Gaines decided to go home to Louisiana in the hope that returning to his roots would allow him to complete his novel.

It worked. Gaines was in Louisiana for six months. And just six months after he returned to San Francisco, the book was completed. Eight months later, his first novel, now titled *Catherine Carmier*, was published. All he had to do now was sit back and see if the nearly five years of work he put into the novel had been worth it.

CATHERINE CARMIER

The book tells the story of a young man, Jackson Guerin, who (like Gaines himself) had left the Louisiana plantation where he had grown up to get an education in California. He returns home to the plantation to visit his beloved Aunt Charlotte, and while there he falls in love with the beautiful Catherine Carmier, the daughter of Raoul, the plantation's manager. During his time there, Jackson rediscovers a world whose inhabitants are defined by their race, by whether they are light skinned or dark skinned, and who are trapped by their own personal and racial history. The conflict between Raoul, who is light skinned and without a son, and Jackson, dark skinned and without a father, is one we will see throughout Gaines's later works.

Despite Gaines's high hopes, reviewers and readers largely ignored *Catherine Carmier*. Those who did review the book noted the young author's obvious talent but faulted him for not directly tackling the racial issues of the day. But direct political discussion was never going to be Gaines's style. Even in his first novel, he preferred to provide the readers with character and dialogue and let any messages about race arise naturally from that, rather than by directly lecturing the reader.

In addition to the lack of critical acclaim, the novel did not bring him the financial success that he had hoped for. And although the book today is praised for the beauty of its prose and for Gaines's subtle handling of its themes, the author himself sees the book's faults as well as anyone.

In its initial drafts, the novel was twice as long as it was in its final form. Like many young and ambitious writers, Gaines tried to put everything into his first effort. It was his editor who told him that there was just too much in the book and encouraged him to cut back and emphasize the book's love story. Despite his efforts, Gaines believes that *Catherine Carmier* "is a very young man's book, a college book in which you try to put everything your instructors have told you to make viewpoint and form right. Later you write with everything you've learned from your reading, from baseball to bars, from all life experience."[6] Valerie Melissa Babb pointed out in her study of Gaines:

> A Gaines more in control of the written medium would later be able to balance such universal themes as love and individual struggle with the more particular themes of his Louisiana setting, but this balance was not fully realized in *Catherine Carmier*. The result is a novel that is somewhat uneven but noteworthy for the masterful rendering of both the physical beauty and the oral traditions of rural Louisiana.[7]

TRYING AGAIN

For the next two years, Gaines tried something new. Instead of writing about Louisiana and its people, he attempted to write about the world in which he was then living: San Francisco and its bohemian artist lifestyle. Gaines actually finished three novels, all set in San Francisco, none of which have been published or ever will be. He has kept them locked away, describing them as perhaps the worst novels ever written by a published author. Despite his love of San Francisco, Gaines found himself unable to write truthfully about his adopted home. Louisiana, with all its racial inequalities and struggles, was still his literary home, his real home.

With the $1,500 advance for *Catherine Carmier* long gone, Gaines again found himself taking on a series of odd jobs. Fortunately, help came to him with the support of a National Endowment for the Arts Study Award. And then his agent won him a two-book contract with Dial Press. But there was a hitch. The editors at Dial wanted to publish a collection of his short stories—his best work to date—but only if he gave them a novel to publish first. Desperate for the money and anxious to get his stories available to a wider audience, Gaines set to work to find the novel he knew was inside him that would please both author and publisher.

Lightning struck when two memories came together to inspire the book. Gaines remembered an incident that occurred on a trip to Louisiana, where he witnessed a knife fight between two young men in a bar. At the same time, the lyrics from Lightnin' Hopkins's classic blues song "Mr. Tim Moore's Farm" kept echoing in his head. These two disparate memories combined to give Gaines the inspiration he needed.

Just seven months later, Gaines had a completed novel, *Of Love and Dust*. The book tells the story of Marcus, a young black man who, instead of being sent to prison, accepts being bonded to a white plantation owner, who

A photo of the blues musician Lightnin' Hopkins. The lyrics from his song "Mr. Tim Moore's Farm" inspired Ernest J. Gaines to write his novel Of Love and Dust.

treats him as his slave. Like Jackson in *Catherine Carmier*, Marcus is a young man without a father or a place in the world. Angry and bitter over what has happened in his life, Marcus takes his revenge on the plantation owner by seducing the man's wife, turning on its head the more common situation of the plantation owner sleeping with his female servants or slaves. The plot of the novel ultimately culminates in murder.

But unlike *Catherine Carmier*, this book came together relatively quickly. Why was that? Part of it, of course, was need: Gaines needed to get the book done and to his publisher as quickly as possible. Part of it was also his intimate understanding of his characters and their situation. As he revealed in a 1969 interview:

> When I brought my young killer to the plantation, I knew the kind of house he would have to live in; I had lived there fifteen years myself. I knew the kind of food he would eat; the same kind that I had eaten. I knew the kind of clothes he would wear, because I had worn the khaki and denim clothes myself. I knew the work he would have to do. I knew the people he would come into contact with day in and day out.[8]

The other reason the book was easier for Gaines to write was purely a technical one. His first novel, *Catherine Carmier*, had been written in the third person. This means that the story is told by a narrator who is not part of the story but who observes and tells the story, knowing everything that the reader needs to know. *Of Love and Dust* is told in the first person, a form that Gaines finds more comfortable and natural. In a first-person narrative, one of the book's characters tells the story in his or her own words. In this case, the story is told through the eyes of Jim Kelly, a plantation tractor driver and friend to Marcus.

While *Of Love and Dust* was not the commercial breakthrough that Gaines had hoped for, it did win the notice of many book reviewers, who gave it generally good reviews. One reviewer described it as "a rare bird, . . . a serious, powerful novel by a talented writer that is accessible to a very wide audience."[9] This aspect of Gaines's work was important to him because he did not want to be perceived as only a black author writing only for black readers, but as a writer who had something to say to readers of all races.

It was Gaines's next book, *Bloodline*, that put him firmly on the literary map. This collection of five of his best short stories gave further evidence that he was a writer to be reckoned with, a writer who mattered. As Babb points out, the collection "can be viewed as a repository of many of the recurring themes Gaines employs in his full-length fiction, for in all, the quest for black manhood, the reverence of the past, and the value of black life emerge as central concerns."[10]

Indeed, the stories are more than just five short stories; they come together, telling the story of a man's life despite not necessarily being about the same character. Gaines elaborated on this in a 1972 interview with John O'Brien:

> The first story is told by a six-year-old child. The second story is told by an eight-year-old child. The third story is by a nineteen-year-old. The fourth story is by someone in his earlier twenties. The final story is told by many characters. I definitely arranged these stories in this order because there is growth. In the first story, "A Long Day in November," a six-year-old child can only see a certain amount of things, he can only interpret a certain amount of things. That's why his story is limited physically to the plantation. By the time he's eight years old in "The Sky Is Gray" it's time for him to

> get out of the quarters. He ends up in a small Southern town where he sees a little bit more. Though he does not understand everything that is going on, he can understand much more than the six-year-old. In "Three Men" the boy is nineteen and has committed murder. Of course, his experiences are much broader than the two boys'. . . . By the time you come to the last story there is much more experience to interpret. You have older women and older men. You have the point of view of the white woman. There are many different experiences coming into the story. So there is constant growth from the first to the last story.[11]

Bloodline, which earned strong reviews upon its publication, has over the years become an acknowledged classic, a collection of stories that has stood the test of time. Indeed, two of the stories, "A Long Day in November" and "The Sky Is Gray," have been recognized as masterpieces. "The Sky Is Gray," in particular, has become one of the most anthologized of contemporary short stories—selected repeatedly for textbooks and short-story collections and praised for the beauty of its prose, the truthfulness of its observations, and the subtlety it shows in depicting the racism faced by the eight-year-old narrator and his mother.

In "The Sky Is Gray," Gaines transforms experience and knowledge into art. The story itself is simple: An eight-year-old boy is suffering from a toothache, and his mother takes him from the plantation where they live to the nearest town to see a dentist. Of course, there is more to the story than that, and Gaines gives the reader a glimpse of an entire world through that one simple incident taken from his own life:

> I had a toothache when I was a child at that age, and I had to ride the bus, just as he rides. At that time, on a bus in the

South, you had a little sign hanging over the aisle and it said "White" on one side and it said "Colored" on the other side, and you had to sit behind that little sign. . . . I also could not eat uptown. There was no place for me to eat; whether it was cold or sleet or rain; and there no place to eat. . . . I also knew about the dentist's waiting room, the cluttered little place that might be full of people waiting to have dental help. Of course, there were all black people in here; the whites were sitting someplace else. So I had gone through all that. This is why I knew what a child would experience. As a writer, I was interpreting the feeling of this child at the time I myself was 30 years old, but I did know the experiences that he would have gone through.[12]

Did you know...

In 1980, a television movie was made of Gaines's short story "The Sky Is Gray." Gaines was not asked to write the screenplay. Instead, Charles Fuller, the playwright best known for his Pulitzer Prize–winning play, *A Soldier's Play*, wrote the script.

Gaines, while understanding that the film was going to be different from his story, was still not altogether pleased with the way it came out, giving it a score of 5 out of 10. What did he object to? To save money, a cornfield was used instead of a cane field. A 13-year-old actor was cast as the lead, instead of the 8-year-old that Gaines had described in the book. And, somewhat surprisingly, throughout the film, the sky is never gray, but blue!

AN IDEA

Despite having two books published in short succession that both received strong reviews, Gaines had still not reached the point where he could live on his writing. After a Rockefeller Grant-in-Aid earned in 1970 gave him a bit more breathing room, Gaines once again began a new novel.

He began playing around with a simple idea that he said came to him while sitting on the porch of his Aunt Augusteen's house at River Lake Plantation. What if, he asked himself, he wrote a "folk biography" that would tell the true story of his people?

He could let several narrators tell the story, the story of one person's life, a life that spanned a hundred years of history. It would include everything he had learned growing up in at River Lake, all the stories, superstitions, and folk tales the old people told while congregating on his Aunt Augusteen's porch on so many evenings. Little did Gaines know that from that idea would emerge the book that is, even today, his best-known and best-loved title—the novel that established Ernest J. Gaines as one of America's best authors.

Actress Cicely Tyson (as Jane Pittman) takes a drink from a "whites only" water fountain in the 1974 made-for-television adaptation of Ernest J. Gaines's novel The Autobiography of Miss Jane Pittman. *Tyson, who portrayed a former slave who lived from the Civil War through the civil rights era, won 2 of the film's 11 Emmy Awards.*

5

Miss Jane Pittman

I had been trying to get Miss Jane Pittman to tell me the story of her life for several years now, but each time I asked her she told me there was no story to tell. I told her she was over a hundred years old, she had been a slave in this country, so there had to be a story. . . .

"What you want know about Miss Jane for?" Mary asked.

"I teach history," I said. "I'm sure her life's story can help me explain things to my students."

"What's wrong with them books you already got?" Mary asked.

"Miss Jane is not in them."[1]

THAT EXCERPT IS FROM the introduction to Gaines's most famous work, *The Autobiography of Miss Jane Pittman*. Of course, the book is a novel. There was no Miss Jane Pittman. But the novel, the story of Jane Pittman's life from slavery through the civil rights movement, is set up as though she were a real person.

Indeed, after the book's publication, several critics wrote reviews describing Miss Jane as a real person. *Newsweek* even asked Gaines to send its editors a photograph of Miss Jane to use in their review. It is a remarkable tribute to Gaines's art that, despite the character being made-up, many readers had believed that this 110-year-old woman had lived and told her story to a professor who wanted to know it.

Although the setup for the novel seems simple enough in hindsight, it took Gaines a good amount of time to arrive at the form best suited to tell Miss Jane's story. After conceiving of Miss Jane's story, Gaines paid a visit to his friend Al Aubert. He began by asking his friend to talk about 12 people or events that a 110-year-old woman who lived between the mid-nineteenth and mid-twentieth centuries would recall. The list itself was fairly straightforward: Abraham Lincoln. The Civil War. The Reconstruction era following the Civil War. The great floods of 1912 and 1927. Baseball. Boxers Jack Johnson and Joe Louis. Jackie Robinson. The Great Depression. President Franklin Delano Roosevelt. Louisiana governor Huey Long. Martin Luther King Jr. The civil rights movement.

Gaines then went to work researching those subjects. He read books by white historians and black historians. He used the archives of Louisiana State University. He went out into the fields and interviewed as many people as he could find, asking them for their memories. But to write his book, he would have to do more than just compile information and then give it directly back to the reader.

Gaines would have to find a way to take the information he had learned and put it into the mind of Miss Jane Pittman, an intelligent but illiterate woman with no formal education. One essential source for Gaines was the book *Lay My Burden Down*, an extraordinary collection of interviews of ex-slaves done by the federal government's Works Progress Administration (WPA, later the Work Projects Administration) during the 1930s. In her study of Ernest Gaines, Valerie Melissa Babb illustrated just how *Lay My Burden Down* gave Gaines the tools he needed to create Jane Pittman's voice. Consider this passage taken from *Lay My Burden Down*:

> When my race first got they freedom and begin to leave they marses, a heap of the marses got raging mad and just tore up truck. They say they gwine kill every n_____ they find. Some of them did do that very thing, boss, sure enough. I's tell you the truth. They shot n______ down by the hundreds. They just wan't gwine let 'em enjoy their freedom. This is the truth, boss.[2]

Now, look at how Gaines takes the interview of former slave Tines Kendricks, uses it for historical information, and then transforms it into the distinctive voice of Jane Pittman:

> The old masters didn't think too much of it at first. They was glad the n______ was leaving. If they got rid of all the bad n______—them the only ones leaving anyhow—if all of them left there wouldn't be no more trouble. They didn't know it at first, but it wasn't just the bad ones leaving. . . . Now, the old masters came back and tried to force the people to stay. They

> turned the Klans looses on them, the Camelias, and the White Brotherhood loose on the people.[3]

FINDING THE FORM

Interestingly, even after Gaines had completed his research and sat down to write, the book's form changed as he worked. Initially, the book was not going to be told in Miss Jane's voice at all. Gaines's first working title for the book was "Sketches of a Plantation," followed by "A Short Biography of Miss Jane Pittman." His original idea for the book was to begin with Pittman's death and then have multiple narrators tell her story—an idea he used in his short story "Just Like a Tree."

This time, however, that approach was not working. Gaines's editor at Dial Press, Bill Decker, suggested to Gaines that he write the book from an autobiographical point of view. At first, Gaines was unable to see exactly what Decker was talking about. Finally, though, he had his "aha" moment and realized that it was Miss Jane's voice that he loved and that it had to be Miss Jane herself who would tell her story. Gaines explained: "I decided to change the way of telling the story because I had fallen in love with my little character, and I thought she could tell the story of her life much better than anyone else. . . . I thought a single voice (Miss Jane's) would keep the story in a straight line."[4]

From that point on, the writing went smoothly. By describing the African-American experience through the eyes and voice of a 110-year-old woman, Gaines gained the freedom to develop the story as he wanted to and as the character of Jane "directed" him to do. "Once the story really got moving, Miss Jane did and said pretty much whatever she wanted, and all I could do was act as her editor, never her advisor."[5]

Gaines elaborated on this idea of a fictional character running away from an author in a 1976 interview with Dan Tooker and Roger Hofheins:

> Lots of times Miss Jane would take over, but I had to have an idea. . . . By the time you get to page 275, if you've really developed the characters well and put them into action, they'll take over, but you have to deal with direction. You must invent some incidents along the way, and when Miss Jane gets into the incident, she'll develop it for you. . . . I just don't sit down without any idea. A novel is like getting on a train to Louisiana. All you know at the moment is that you're getting on the train, and you're going to Louisiana. But you don't know

Did you know...

Outside of writing and literature, Gaines's other major artistic passion is for music. Jazz, blues, classical—he loves it all. But did you know that Gaines selects specific music to listen to based on the book that he is writing at the time?

For example, while writing *The Autobiography of Miss Jane Pittman*, the key piece of music for Gaines was Modest P. Mussorgsky's masterpiece for piano and orchestra, *Pictures at an Exhibition*. The work, which uses music to describe a series of paintings on display by Russian artist Viktor Hartmann, inspired Gaines's own work on *Miss Jane*, which he originally envisioned as a series of sketches of a Louisiana plantation. Gaines estimates that while working on the book, he listened to *Pictures at an Exhibition* every day for two years!

> what the conductor is going to look like; you don't know who you're going to sit behind, or in front of, or beside; you don't know what the weather is going to be when you pass through certain areas of the country; you don't know what's going to happen South; you don't know all these things, but you know you're going to Louisiana. You know you're going by train, and that it's going to take so many hours, days.[6]

A CRITICAL SUCCESS

The journey was worth it. *The Autobiography of Miss Jane Pittman*, dedicated in part "to the memory of My beloved aunt, Miss Augusteen Jefferson, who did not walk a day in her life but who taught me the importance of standing,"[7] was published in 1971 to rapturous reviews. Geoffrey Wolff wrote in *Newsweek*: "Gaines' novel brings to mind other great works: *The Odyssey* for the way his heroine's travels manage to summarize the American history of her race, and *Huckleberry Finn* for the clarity of her voice, for her rare capacity to sort through all the mess of years and things to find the one true story in it all."[8] A reviewer for the *New York Times* believed "this grand, robust, most valuable novel . . . is impossible to dismiss or put down."[9] Josh Greenfield, writing in *Life*, noted:

> Never mind that [the book] . . . offered up in the form of taped reminiscences is artifice. The effect is stunning. [It exudes] a refreshing mix of wit and wrath, imagination and indignation, misery and poetry. And I can recall no more memorable female character in Southern fiction since Lena of Faulkner's *Light in August* than Miss Jane Pittman herself.[10]

Can you imagine how thrilled Ernest Gaines must have been to be compared to one of his own favorite authors, William Faulkner?

The book became a national best seller, both in hardcover and later as a paperback. Based on the novel's incredible popularity, CBS purchased the television rights for *The Autobiography of Miss Jane Pittman* for $50,000. The TV movie achieved blockbuster ratings and critical raves when it was first broadcast in 1974, and it went on to sweep that year's Emmy Awards, including awards for best actress, director, screenwriter, and music.

Ironically, the creator of Miss Jane Pittman had nothing to do with the TV movie. Although he was on the set as an adviser during shooting, another man, Tracy Keenan Winn, wrote the screenplay. It seems likely Gaines would have had difficulty cutting the scope of his novel down to fit into the time restraints of a two-hour film. Yet given those restraints, he was pleased with the results, although he has said he believes that today more people remember the film than they do the book itself. While that is probably not correct, it is true that even today, decades after the book's publication, *The Autobiography of Miss Jane Pittman* is the book most closely connected with the author's name. The novel's success finally gave Gaines the recognition that he had so long sought. As he said in an interview in 1982 with Jeanie Blake, "*Miss Jane* carried me on her back for a long time."[11]

And it was *Miss Jane* who lifted Gaines into the upper echelon of American authors. But now, after the years of struggle had finally eased, he had a new problem. With the success of *The Autobiography of Miss Jane Pittman*, critics and readers alike would be expecting another masterpiece from him. It would take another seven years before another book by Gaines reached the nation's bookstores and libraries.

Ernest J. Gaines is shown during an interview in his San Francisco home on April 12, 1977, just before the publication of In My Father's House *in 1978.*

6

Gathering the Old Men

I hope when I die they won't put on my tombstone, "He wrote Miss Jane Pittman.*" Put anything else, but don't put just that.*[1]

—Ernest J. Gaines

WHILE MOST AUTHORS hope that they will write a book that "clicks" with the reading public and becomes a best seller, such success can also become a kind of curse. Not only does that kind of success put pressure on the author to achieve the same mix of critical and popular acclaim, but there is always concern in the author's mind that he or she will never be able to duplicate that success—thus, Gaines's fear that he will forever be known as just the author of *The Autobiography of Miss Jane Pittman*.

The book's success, however, was a godsend to Gaines. He received a number of awards, including a Guggenheim Fellowship, the California Commonwealth Gold Medal Award, the Louisiana Library Association Award, and the Black Academy of Arts and Letters Award, in addition to the book being named a Notable Book by the American Library Association. (He was also short-listed for both the Pulitzer Prize and the National Book Award but lost to his old teacher, Wallace Stegner, for the Pulitzer and to Flannery O'Connor, who won the National Book Award posthumously for her *Collected Short Stories*.)

In addition, the money earned from *Miss Jane Pittman* allowed him to move from his small apartment to a larger, eight-room flat on Divisadero Street in a working-class neighborhood of San Francisco. There, surrounded by his ever-growing library (by 1974, he already owned approximately 7,000 books) and his collection of jazz, blues, and classical records, Gaines settled in to work on his next book.

IN MY FATHER'S HOUSE

Most people who have a job follow a schedule. Get up in the morning, get ready for the day, go to work, do your job, and come home. For Ernest Gaines, being an author is very similar. The only difference is that his home is also his place of work.

Beginning work on his new book, he followed the same schedule he had for years and which he continues to follow today: Get up at 6:30 or 7:00 in the morning, eat a little breakfast, go for a walk, then sit down and get to work. And just as he did when he was just 16 and trying to write the first novel, Gaines writes everything out in pencil in longhand. It is only then that he types it out and then types it out again, revising every step of the way. For Gaines, like most authors, it is through rewriting that he is able to achieve exactly what he wants to achieve in his work. Gaines described the process in a 1983 interview with Mary Ellen Doyle:

> I rewrite a lot. Dialogue is very easy for me to write; I can write, say, ten pages of it a day. Of course, I may rewrite it ten times to get it exactly the way I want it, but I can revise dialogue very fast. Descriptive passages give me some problem; I might write only one page of descriptive work a day. How much work I can do in any day's time depends on what the situation is, whether I have a group of people I'm writing about, or one or two people talking or moving, what part of a scene I'm doing. Instead of trying to write a certain number of pages or a certain amount of words a day, I try to get in a certain amount of time a day—about five hours. I start at nine in the morning and work until about two in the afternoon. I stop in the middle for coffee or water, but I try to get in that much time each day, five days a week. If I get two pages today, maybe I get five pages the next day, and the next day only two or three paragraphs. It depends on the problem of the book that I'm working out.[2]

It turned out that problems in writing his next book were wide ranging. Initially, he began working on a piece titled "The House and the Field." When that effort reached a dead end, he put it aside and began work on what would become his fourth novel, *In My Father's House*. It would take him seven years to write.

Why did it take so long? He had difficulties working out the themes. He had problems with character development. As he said in a 1991 interview, "I just didn't know how. . . .

But, it was also a book I felt I had to write. It's a father/son thing and that's one of the themes in most of my novels. The black father looking for the son or the son looking for the father."[3] He also had difficulties coming up with an ending, telling interviewer Jeanie Blake, "I bet I wrote six, seven different endings for *In My Father's House*. I had everybody dying off in it. I just didn't know what to do with it."[4]

He also had difficulty with the point of view. Like his first novel, *Catherine Carmier*, *In My Father's House* had to be told from a third-person, omniscient point of view. Although Gaines has no problem writing dialogue, whether writing in the first or third person, other things, such as description, narration, and working out themes are difficult for him to do in the third person. Gaines sees himself as a storyteller, and he wants his readers to look at the character telling the story from the first-person point of view as an actual person who is relating a story. The difference for Gaines is simple: "When you're dealing with the omniscient point of view, you are not being told a story, you are reading a story."[5] For a natural storyteller such as Gaines, the difference is crucial. Despite the difficulties, Gaines was glad he wrote the novel. He explained:

> It's a book I had to write because I was haunted by the idea. It cost me more time (seven years) and pain than any other book I've written. It is the story of a minister and his son, one of the children he'd fathered as a young man but never even seen in the many years since their mother left him. Until he left God, this was just "something that happened," that happened to many Black males then. When he realized his responsibility, he tried to make it up by becoming the "new man" with a new family, and still forgot the old. When the past catches up, he goes to God for an answer but finds it can't be fixed in a few

> days. There is an old Negro saying, "God isn't always there when you call him, but he's always on time." But this Christian belief is shaken, cracked. God helped the minister to help other people, but when he needed God to bring himself and his son together, God failed.[6]

Is it possible that part of Gaines's difficulty in writing *In My Father's House* was because he was thinking of his own father, who had abandoned him at such an early age?

Much to Gaines's disappointment, when *In My Father's House* was finally published in 1978, it turned out to be both a critical and popular failure. The only money that Gaines earned from the book was the $20,000 advance he was given at the beginning of the writing process. After taking into account taxes and the money due to his agent, Gaines made approximately $2,000 a year over the seven years it took to write *In My Father's House*. Even with his earnings from *The Autobiography of Miss Jane Pittman*, Gaines once again found himself under serious financial pressure.

Since 1971, when Gaines accepted a position as writer in residence at Denison University in Granville, Ohio, he had supplemented his income by accepting the same position at a number of other colleges and universities, including the University of Arkansas and Whittier College. These sporadic assignments did not provide him with the economic security he wanted and needed. Fortunately, Gaines received an offer from the University of Southwestern Louisiana (USL), located approximately 40 miles (64 kilometers) from the plantation where he grew up, which seemed to be the answer to his prayers. He explained:

> I came down in '81 and spent a year, and they asked me if I would come down every year for one semester, and I said

> okay. At the same time, the University of Houston asked me to do the same thing, to teach one semester on alternate years, and I thought I could teach one semester at Houston on one year and one semester at USL on the next. I could write the rest of the time.[7]

Without having to worry about how he was going to pay his bills, Gaines settled into his new arrangement: teaching English one semester and spending the other half of the year working on what would be his next book.

A GATHERING OF OLD MEN

The plot of his next novel is simple and tragic: Set in 1979 on the Marshall Plantation, *A Gathering of Old Men* opens with Candy Marshall, part owner of the plantation, asking a young boy, George Elliot Jr. (known as Snookum), to deliver some messages for her. The African-American men still on the plantation, all elderly, are to come with 12-gauge shotguns and newly shot number-five shells to Mathu's house. Candy is certain that Mathu, an elderly black man who helped to raise her, has shot Beau Boutan, a Cajun farmer who leased land on the plantation. (Cajuns are people of French descent who live primarily in Louisiana and in parts of Texas.)

In order to protect Mathu from being arrested and going to trial, Candy decides to confess to the murder and enlists the other elderly black men to confess to the murder as well. With everyone pleading guilty and numerous empty shotgun shells around, she hopes it will prove impossible for the police to arrest Mathu for the crime. There is one other major plot element: Candy, as well as everyone else in the story, is certain that the Boutan family will take matters into their own hands and seek revenge for Beau's death before law enforcement officials can settle the case.

Ernest J. Gaines's novel **A Gathering of Old Men** *was adapted for film in 1987 and starred Louis Gossett Jr.* **(in foreground).**

That is the plot. But what the book is really about is the group of elderly African-American men who confront Sheriff Mapes on the porch and front lawn of Mathu's home. In the book, the men recall their pasts, all the times when they were subordinate to white men, and decide finally, for the first time in their lives, to stand up and be recognized as men. As Gaines pointed out: "The old men as a group are the protagonist. The central motif is that they had not acted manfully in the past, and here was God giving them a second chance to stand up one day."[8]

The plot and themes of the book are, as you can see, fairly basic. The art of the book is in the telling, and it was the decision of just how to tell the story that helped make the book the contemporary classic that it is. After the difficulties that Gaines had in writing *In My Father's House*, it should come as no surprise that he decided early on to write the book from the first-person point of view. One person within the story, he felt, should be the one who tells the story. The question was: Which character would it be?

Originally, the story was going to be told by Lou Dimes, a friend of Candy's, a "liberal white guy" and newspaper reporter who is called to witness the events at Mathu's house. Gaines pointed out in an interview with Elsa Saeta and Izora Skinner in 1991:

> I started originally not from the omniscient point of view, not from the third person point of view, but from the single point of view. Lou Dimes tells the whole thing. But I found that he could not tell the story itself like I wanted it told because he could not see the little boy running down the street banging his butt and he couldn't see Janey inside the house talking to herself and he couldn't see many of the other characters. He could not reveal their inner thinking to the audience as they could themselves. I went from his single point of view to the multiple point of view because I didn't want to go back to the omniscient. I feel trapped in the omniscient. . . . I feel much freer and I think my narratives flow more smoothly with the first person or the multiple point of view.[9]

So once again, after trying out a point of view that prevented him from telling the story that he wanted to tell, Gaines changed it. *A Gathering of Old Men* would still be in the first person, but with multiple characters telling the story. But interestingly, it is not the characters who are most involved in the plot—Mathu, Candy, Fix, Charlie—who tell the story. It is people on the outside—Janey,

Did you know...

In 1987, Gaines's novel *A Gathering of Old Men* was adapted into a television movie. And once again, Gaines was less than thrilled with the final result.

To fit a 200-page novel into the time constraints of a 90-minute TV movie, changes were made. The number of "old men" was drastically cut. Characters were combined, with dialogue taken from two or three different characters and given to just one. Sheriff Mapes, described in the book as a large, imposing man, was played by a smaller, thin one. The book's humor was gone. Even the book's ending, an explosion of violence that is necessary to the plot and theme, was altered.

Over the years, Gaines has grown philosophical about the changes that occur when a book is made into a film. He tells a story about the composer Johannes Brahms to illustrate his point. On one occasion, Brahms heard one of his concertos being played by a gypsy orchestra. When the piece ended, someone asked Brahms what he thought of it. Brahms responded: "Well, so it can be done like that. I didn't know that." Gaines feels the same way about the films made from his books. It is a different medium and a different take on what he originally put down on paper. Who knew, he feels, that you could make that particular movie out of his book?

Snookum, the white people at the store, and the old men themselves—who tell their stories and, through them, the book's plot.

It is important to note that although the book is a powerful demonstration of injustices against blacks and the need to stand up against those injustices, the book is not a one-sided attack on whites. The book is a powerful novel, in which each and every character is allowed his or her own moment of humanity. They are fictional yet real people; both sides are depicted as flawed, living and struggling with racism. Even the book's nominal villains are presented as human beings, because, as Gaines said, "It's a normal thing; I think Klansmen could love their children. For me to be fair as a writer, I cannot deny Fix or Will his humanity, and I don't know anyone totally without feeling."[10]

The book was published in 1983 to nearly unanimous praise and strong sales. After the perceived disappointment of *In My Father's House*, reviewers were happy to welcome Gaines home to the Louisiana plantation life he knew so well. A reviewer for the *Los Angeles Herald-Examiner* cheered: "Gaines writes with humor, a strong sense of drama and a compassionate understanding of people who find themselves in opposing positions. . . . Not least, he knows how to tell a story, and *A Gathering of Old Men* is a good one."[11]

Reynolds Price, another great Southern writer, praised Gaines in the *New York Times Book Review*:

> In *A Gathering of Old Men* Gaines has built, with large and single-minded skills, a dignified and calamitous and perhaps finally comic pageant to summarize the history of an enormous, long waste in our past—the mindless, mutual hatred of white and black, which, he implies, may be slowly heal-

> ing. . . . Mr. Gaines' unflagging commitment is to a breadth, even grandeur, of grasp and comprehensiveness.[12]

The praise soon spread worldwide. In the London *Daily Telegraph*, a reviewer thought that Gaines's story was "so tense, so fresh and penetrating that we are kept on edge from beginning to end. . . . The tension is admirably maintained and in-depth characterization achieved by using various people as mouthpieces."[13]

Perhaps the review that best sums up Gaines's achievement came in the August 1983 issue of *Library Journal*:

> After the first two pages this new novel . . . moves along as briskly as any reader would wish. . . . The narrative is passed like a baton from character to character as each successive chapter is related by a different person. Although the tone occasionally becomes a trifle exalted, the fictional world created in this book is mesmerizing.[14]

The critical success of *A Gathering of Old Men* reestablished Gaines's reputation as one of America's finest writers. He would now be entering into a period filled with success, security, and a surprising change in his personal life.

A photo of the electric chair used at Louisiana State Prison. In writing A Lesson Before Dying, *Ernest J. Gaines explored many of his familiar literary themes in a death-row prison setting.*

7

Teaching and Marriage

IN 1983, THE UNIVERSITY of Southwestern Louisiana (USL) offered Gaines tenure. He finally had a permanent teaching position: After teaching at USL in the fall, he would return to San Francisco for the spring and summer to write. For him at that time, it was the best of all possible worlds.

But he was not only offered a tenured teaching position. Gaines was now a prime catch for any university: a talented writer and teacher whose books were both critical and popular successes. The people of Lafayette, Louisiana, in both the university and business communities, were determined that he should stay in Lafayette, lending them and their school literary prestige. For the previous two years, while Gaines had been teaching at USL, he had been forced to live on campus in Cajun Village, a housing area designed for married students.

When Gaines returned to USL in August 1983, he was surprised at the airport by some of his colleagues in the English Department and driven to the stately residential area of Arbolada, where he was given the keys to a beautiful old brick home. That home, previously owned by the Mouton family, was now to be his permanent home for as long as he remained on the USL faculty. It has been speculated that the Moutons' generosity was inspired by their young son, who, after watching the movie *The Autobiography of Miss Jane Pittman*, had talked about nothing else for five days. Mouton said, "For the story to have that kind of impact on a young white boy in the South, it had to be exceptional."[1] A letter written to Gaines from the Moutons simply stated: "Please accept the gift of this home in honor of Miss Jane, Catherine, and all the Old Men."[2]

Gaines quickly settled into the comfortable pattern of his new life: teaching at "home" in Louisiana, then returning "home" to San Francisco to write. Gaines enjoyed teaching because it gave him the opportunity to work with aspiring writers and pass on to them what he had learned during his long career. It does raise a question, however: Does Gaines believe that someone can become a writer by taking creative writing classes?

The answer, which may surprise you, is a definite "no." Gaines feels that writers cannot be made in class. The aspiring writer has to come to class with more than a pencil, paper, and the desire to be a writer. To write, one must be armed not only with the desire to be a writer but also with a life that you can draw on in your work. Gaines also

One of Ernest J. Gaines's inspirations has been the work of the novelist and short-story writer Eudora Welty, who is shown here on March 29, 1955. Welty received the Howells Medal of the American Academy of Arts and Letters for her 1954 novel The Ponder Heart.

believes you need to be a reader as well. It was his teachers at San Francisco State and at Stanford who taught him that, saying:

> "You want to write . . . then write, but these are the books we recommend that can help you understand what literature is. Read—not only Faulkner and Hemingway—but read everybody else—read Twain, read Chekhov, read Joyce, read everybody." Reading to see how these authors [Cather, Hemingway, Faulkner] put their stories together helped me develop my characters, plot, use of dialogue, and use of humor.[3]

Take for example one of Gaines's most famous stories, "The Sky Is Gray." Gaines is the first to acknowledge that he probably would not have been able to write that story if he had not first read Eudora Welty's short story "A Worn Path." Welty's tale of an old woman going into town to get medicine for a sick child had a direct influence on his story of a mother taking her child into town to go to the dentist. Welty showed Gaines that a story about a journey may end up being about more than just the journey. As Gaines said in an interview for the *New Orleans Review*, "There's no plagiarism or anything involved. But since you can't write out of a void, you need some crutch somewhere; you need somebody to say ok this is one route you can take."[4]

To Gaines, learning to write means learning how to read and then using what one has learned in order to write and find one's own voice. What he gained from his own creative writing classes was having a professor read what he wrote and tell him exactly what was working and what was not. He recalled his professor saying,

> Good here . . . build here . . . take all this out here . . . you're becoming too Faulknerian here . . . too much like Hemingway

over here . . . you need to find and use your own voice . . . you have it in you and you can only do it by rewriting the work . . . you have to go over it and go over it and go over it again.[5]

Gaines tried to impart these lessons to his own students. To be a writer, he would tell them, you have to have something to say. All he could do as an instructor was to help

Did you know...

There are very few American writers who have not been influenced one way or another by Ernest Hemingway, the Nobel Prize–winning twentieth-century author. Some see his prose style—terse sentences without one unneeded word—as a model to use in their own writing. Others look at what he did and, anxious to escape his influence, move in the other direction, writing a more elegant and artistic prose. For some writers, such as Norman Mailer for example, Hemingway's prose and life, with his emphasis on passing life's tests with grace, provides them with a goal for their own lives. Others, appalled by what they see as Hemingway's constant need to prove his masculinity, go the other way.

However one is influenced by Ernest Hemingway, his short stories; novels such as *A Farewell to Arms*, *The Sun Also Rises*, and *The Old Man and the Sea*; and the memoir *A Moveable Feast* have played and continue to play a part in the intellectual and emotional development of generations of American writers.

bring it out of them. And the lessons he had learned so many years earlier that he was now passing along to his students were lessons he used himself as he settled in to work on his next book, one that would be acclaimed as one of his greatest and earn him a form of literary recognition that had so far eluded him.

A LESSON BEFORE DYING

Gaines began working on his next novel, *A Lesson Before Dying*, in the mid-1980s. In the course of interviews during this time, he would be asked about his new project, but he was reluctant to talk about something still in its early stages. "I don't usually talk about it," he said. "This is where you get all the ohs and the ahs when you're trying to say something that you really don't understand yet."[6] As we have seen, in book after book, Gaines was likely to change the book's point of view or direction as it was being written. How could he talk intelligently about something when he was unsure where "the journey," as he called it, was going to take him?

Once again, the journey began in Louisiana, where Gaines used the story of a crime to explore one of his favorite themes: What does it mean to be a man in a society that tries to keep African-American men from being men? In the novel, a young black man named Jefferson has been convicted of a murder he may or may not have committed and sentenced to death in the electric chair. The story's other main character, Grant Wiggins, is a young man from the same plantation who had left to complete his education and has recently returned to be the plantation's new teacher. Grant has been asked by Jefferson's godmother to talk with him and help him become a "man" before he is executed.

Gaines's interest is not in the fairness of the legal system that convicted Jefferson but in the search for self-respect and awareness under unfair conditions. One of Gaines's favorite writers, Ernest Hemingway, wrote often of the value of "grace under pressure," which became one of Gaines's main themes as well—the idea of bravely facing whatever pressures one may endure. Grant's assignment is not to save Jefferson's life but to convince him that he is a man and not the "hog" he was described as being by his own lawyer in the course of his trial.

As is often the case, the book went through a series of changes during the writing. Gaines had originally intended to set his book in 1988. But when he was unable to receive an answer from the warden of Louisiana's Angola Prison as to whether or not a teacher would be allowed to visit a death-row inmate, he decided to change the story back to 1948, the year before Gaines himself left for California and the year in which many of his books take place. This change alone made it a different novel from the one he had originally envisioned; it allowed him to write about a period in which racism was open and accepted.

Even though the book is a work of fiction, Gaines again carefully researched the book as he went along. Time was spent talking to lawyers and sheriffs and gathering the details on such things as Louisiana's portable electric chair and the time and day of all state executions. He wanted the book to be believable and "real" within the confines of the novel format.

And again, as he wrote, Gaines played around with point of view. The teacher, Grant Wiggins, largely narrates the novel. But at the end of the novel, the reader also gets to read the journal that Jefferson has kept his last days in prison. And finally, on the day of the prisoner's execution, the novel shifts temporarily from first-person narrative to the third person, allowing the reader to witness the reactions of a wide spectrum of the local community to the event, both for and against.

It is interesting to note that when Gaines started work on *A Lesson Before Dying* in 1988, he was uncertain whether or not Jefferson would be executed at the book's conclusion. Gaines considered the possibility that the governor would pardon Jefferson, but after interviewing an attorney, he knew how the book had to end. Gaines said: "After he described that tarpaulin-covered truck delivering that [electric] chair and generator on an early foggy morning, I knew I had no other ending but that Jefferson would be executed. I wanted the reader to see that truck and that chair and to hear that generator."[7]

A Lesson Before Dying was published in 1993 to rave reviews. In an exerpt of a review reprinted on the cover of the novel's paperback edition, the *Chicago Tribune* declares, "This majestic, moving novel is an instant classic, a book that will be read, discussed and taught beyond the rest of our lives."[8] In addition to rave reviews, the book went on to capture the 1993 National Book Critics Circle Award for Fiction, one of America's most prestigious literary awards. In 1997, Oprah Winfrey selected it for her book club, encouraging millions of her fans, many of whom had likely never heard of Ernest J. Gaines, to read his work for the first time.

A VERY GOOD YEAR

Overall, 1993 was a very good year for Gaines, both professionally and personally. You may have noticed that throughout this book there has been little discussion of Gaines's personal life or of the women in his life. Of course, he went on dates. But for the majority of his life, writing was his life, and he was prepared to devote himself to it completely. In a 1993 interview with Ruth Laney, he recalled:

> Many of the kids I went to school with at State, or at Stanford, couldn't take it [the writing life]. They got married, had families, started teaching, started businesses. But maybe, at the same time, they didn't have a damned thing to write about in the first place. Because I think if you have something to write about and really want to do it, you'll give up everything. If you want to be a writer, you don't love anybody else but your writing. You're married to it. You have to have the kind of ego, to believe that you have something to say that no one else can say. You will not let anything in the world get in the way of it.[9]

This is not to say that Gaines did not have regrets about focusing solely on his writing. Over the holidays especially, while visiting his own brothers and sisters and seeing their children, he was sorry not to have had children of his own. Yet he felt he had no real choice. "I knew darned well I had to be a writer. I could not afford to have a child around, because I would not have been able to support that child. I had to write."[10]

As his finances stabilized, Gaines found himself in a position where he could finally have a writing life and a personal life as well. In 1988, while appearing at the Miami International Book Fair, he was approached for an autograph by Dianne Saulney, a Louisiana native who worked as an assistant district attorney in Miami. There was an immediate spark between the two, and for the next year and a half, they exchanged letters without actually seeing each other in person. For their first date, the two met at her sister's house in New Orleans, watching videotapes of a family wedding. Later, they went out for coffee and beignets (a kind of New Orleans doughnut) and talked. Gaines and Saulney, who had previously been married and was the mother of adult children, felt immediately comfortable with each other's company.

Five years later, in May 1993, the couple married. For Gaines, it was just a question of the right woman at the right time. "We have a very close relationship. I keep telling Dianne we've been married for thirty-three years, because this relationship is the one I dreamed of when I was writing *Catherine Carmier*."[11] Everything was falling into place. Gaines was living the life he had always wanted, a life where he could "just sit around and talk to them [students] maybe once or twice a week. And that was before I ever knew that there would be a woman in my life, or who that woman would be. And now there's Dianne. What frightens me is that so many things are falling into place."[12]

Little did Gaines know that there was one more part of the puzzle about to fall into place, one that would add to Gaines's reputation and ease any financial problems he might have once and for all.

Ernest J. Gaines is photographed on March 27, 1996. Since winning the John D. and Catherine T. MacArthur Foundation Fellowship in 1993, the author has had the financial security to continue to explore his art.

8

Security

Whenever too much good happens, I'm afraid. I hate to be pessimistic, but I think that life is balance. A lot of people are saying, "You deserve this; you've never received this kind of recognition before." But I'm getting so much now. And some kind of way, the Old Man balances.[1]

—Ernest J. Gaines

THE YEAR 1993 WAS turning out to be an excellent one for Ernest J. Gaines. His seventh book, *A Lesson Before Dying*, had been published to critical acclaim, had received the National Book Critics Circle Award, and was selling well. At the age of 60, he had married for the first time. And finally, in June 1993, Gaines received an award that, while unexpected, was entirely welcome.

Beginning in 1981, the John D. and Catherine T. MacArthur Foundation established the MacArthur Fellows Program, which presents MacArthur Fellowships (nicknamed the Genius Awards) to 20 to 40 U.S. citizens per year working in any field who "show exceptional merit and promise for continued and enhanced creative work."[2]

According to the foundation's Web site, "the fellowship is not a reward for past accomplishment, but rather an investment in a person's originality, insight, and potential."[3] The award, which is now worth $500,000, is paid out in quarterly installments over a five-year period. There is no application for the award. People are anonymously nominated by a body of nominators who give their recommendations to a small committee of about a dozen people, also anonymous. This committee reviews each nominee and then passes their recommendations to the president and board of directors. Most MacArthur fellows only learn that they have been considered when they receive their congratulatory phone call.

Gaines was in his Miami condo (he had begun splitting his time between Louisiana and Florida after his marriage) when he received the news. The telephone call had originally gone to USL, which had been told by Gaines not to give out his phone number except in the case of an emergency. After several confused calls back and forth between the MacArthur Committee, USL, and Gaines, the author finally returned the MacArthur Committee's call, convinced that they were calling him to ask for a recommendation. He recalled:

> Finally I spoke to the person, and she said, "Mr. Gaines, we finally got you. Congratulations, you are a MacArthur

> Fellow." And I thought, "Oh God! That's what you've been calling about?" And the next thing I said was, "How much do I get?" [Laughter] They had a hard time getting in touch with me to give me this money! What my wife and I are doing is putting it in the bank—we didn't buy a yacht! We didn't buy a Rolls Royce, or quit our jobs. And she's still an attorney in Miami, and I'm still teaching at USL.[4]

With a MacArthur Award then totaling $355,000, Gaines could worry less about earning money and concentrate on the things that mattered to him: writing and teaching.

GIVING SOMETHING BACK

With the prize money in hand, Gaines now had the freedom to focus solely on graduate students at the University of Southwestern Louisiana and sought to pass on to them the lessons he had learned over the course of his career.

Because he selects his own students based on their previous work, he knows that they are already passionate about writing when they come to him. His job is not to teach them how to write but how to do it better. He usually teaches just one night a week for about three hours. Gaines and his students sit at a round table, and the students read their work aloud to the entire class in turn. The "teaching" is in the discussion of the work, as Gaines and the other students look at what an individual student has written and talk about it. For an aspiring writer, it is an invaluable education. Gaines noted:

> You have the opinion of 13–14 people who are at the same level as the student plus mine as someone who knows something about writing, someone who has been at the work for a while, someone who's done a lot of reading, someone who's read all kinds of manuscripts. I've been reading manuscripts

> for I don't know how many years and so I have a feeling for what a story should be like. But I always tell the writer "you have to take it all with a grain of salt—you must be your harshest critic—you must do it." I help them with their craft. . . . I have students in my classes whom I think I've helped . . . they've had things published and I think I've had something to do with it.[5]

COMING FULL CIRCLE

In addition to earning a MacArthur Fellowship, Gaines continued to receive recognition for his extraordinary contributions to American literature. In 2000 alone, Gaines received the National Humanities Medal, the Louisiana Writer Award, the National Governors' Arts Award, membership in the prestigious American Academy of Arts and Letters, and was made a Chevalier of France's Order of Arts and Letters.

An honor that Gaines is particularly proud of first occurred in 2007, when the Baton Rouge Area Foundation began presenting the Ernest J. Gaines Award to young writers. According to the foundation's Web site, the award, consisting of $10,000 and a commemorative sculpture, is presented annually "to recognize the best newly published African American writers from across the country" and is intended to "inspire and recognize African-American writers of excellence as they work to achieve the literary heights for which Ernest J. Gaines is known."[6]

But although Gaines could easily have settled into his role as a richly rewarded "grand old man" of American literature, he was not content to rest on his laurels. In 2005, Gaines published *Mozart and Leadbelly*, a collection of essays, short stories, speeches, and interviews.

Did you know...

Shortly after Ernest Gaines became writer in residence at the University of Southwestern Louisiana (USL) in 1983, he was asked about the location of his original manuscripts. Gaines responded that they were being stored in several old trunks in San Francisco.

No longer. In the spring of 2008, USL (now known as the University of Louisiana, Lafayette) announced that those manuscripts would become the foundation of a newly established International Center for Ernest Gaines Studies, which will be built on the third floor of the Dupre Library.

The center will become the repository of all of Gaines's papers and will include original manuscripts, handwritten drafts, books, journal articles, and a collection of translations of Gaines's books. In addition, the center will coordinate Gaines research—there are plans to conduct an Ernest J. Gaines Scholars Conference in the spring of 2010. In the words of Marcia Gaudet, head of the school's English Department, "The availability of the author's papers will provide students with the workings of literary genius."*

---

* "Home for Good: Author's Work Will Be Preserved in New Center in Dupre Library." *La Louisiane*, Spring 2008. http://www.louisiana.edu/Advancement/PRNS/lala/2008-Spring/gainescenter.pdf.

In the essays, including "Miss Jane and I," "Aunty and the Black Experience in Louisiana," and "Writing *A Lesson Before Dying*," Gaines looks back at his career and talks about the people, places, and events that helped him to become a writer. He also included for the first time in book form several of his earliest works: "The Turtles" and "Boy in the Double-Breasted Suit"—the two stories he submitted to Stanford in 1957 when applying for a writing fellowship. For Gaines, the book was an obvious opportunity to look back at his career and let the reader know what made him a writer and why, after so many years, Louisiana is still home, and why it has remained the place he has always wanted to write about. He remarked:

> I wanted to smell that Louisiana earth, feel that Louisiana sun, sit under the shade oaks, search for pecans in that Louisiana grass in one of those Louisiana yards next to one of those Louisiana bayous, not far from a Louisiana river. I wanted to see on paper those Louisiana black children walking to school on cold days while yellow Louisiana school buses passed them by. I wanted to see on paper those black parents going to work before the sun came up and coming back after the sun went down.[7]

In a way, despite having lived for years in San Francisco, and then splitting his time between Louisiana and San Francisco, and then Louisiana and Miami, Gaines had never left Louisiana. No matter where he lived, it was and always would be his home.

And now it is his permanent home. Ernest Gaines is again living full time in Louisiana. In a twist that Gaines could probably never have anticipated, and that would seem a bit unbelievable in a novel, he and his wife are living in a new house they built in Pointe Coupee Parish, on land that was once part of River Lake Plantation, the very plantation where he had grown up and where his ancestors had labored for generations, first as slaves, then as sharecroppers.

Ernest J. Gaines was able to return to his ancestral home, but unlike many of his own fictional characters, he was able to do so on his own terms. He did so as one of America's most respected authors, the man who had taken a corner of Louisiana where he had grown up, and which he had both loved and hated, and through the power of his writing made it his own. Louisiana made him the writer that he became, and through his writings, readers are able to see the African-American experience in Louisiana through the eyes of Ernest Gaines. As Gaines said:

> I think one of the greatest things that has happened to me, as a writer and as a human being, is that I was born in the South, that I was born in Louisiana. . . . I think that Louisiana is probably the most romantic and interesting of all southern states—the land, the language, the colors, the bayous, the fields—all these things together, the combination of all these things, I think, make it an extremely interesting place. If I were to come from any southern state, I think Louisiana is the one that I could choose. And I'm glad I'm from here. I'm glad I came from here.[8]

CHRONOLOGY

1933 Ernest James Gaines is born January 15 on River Lake Plantation in Oscar, Pointe Coupee Parish, Louisiana.

1941 While attending a one-room school, Gaines begins to work in the fields, earning 50 cents a day for his efforts.

1945 Gaines attends St. Augustine Middle School for Catholic African-American children.

1948 Gaines leaves Louisiana to join his mother and new stepfather in California; his spare time is spent reading in the local public library.

1949 He writes his first novel, an early version of *Catherine Carmier*; when a New York publisher rejects it, he burns the manuscript.

1951 Gaines graduates from high school and enters Vallejo Junior College.

1953 After he graduates from Vallejo Junior College, he spends the next two years in the U.S. Army, stationed at Guam.

1955 He enrolls at San Francisco State College.

1957 Gaines graduates from San Francisco State College; two of his stories, "Boy in the Double-Breasted Suit" and "The Turtles," are published in the school's literary journal, *Transfer*, where they catch the eye of Dorothea Oppenheimer, who will become his literary agent until her death in 1987.

1958 He wins a Wallace Stegner award and studies at Stanford University in the Creative Writing Department.

1963 Having trouble working on his first novel, Gaines returns to Louisiana for a six-month visit.

1964 Gaines's first novel, *Catherine Carmier*, is published.

1967 Gaines's second novel, *Of Love and Dust*, is published; he wins the National Endowment for the Arts Study Award.

1968 *Bloodline*, a collection of five of Gaines's short stories, is published.

1970 He receives a Rockefeller Grant-in-Aid.

1971 *The Autobiography of Miss Jane Pittman*, Gaines's third novel and greatest success to date, is published; *A Long Day in November* is published as a children's book.

1972–1974 He begins work on fourth novel; he receives a Guggenheim Fellowship, the California Commonwealth Gold Medal Award, the Louisiana Library Association Award, and the Black Academy of Arts and Letters Award for *Miss Jane*.

1978 *In My Father's House*, Gaines's fourth novel, is published.

1981 He begins teaching each fall term at the University of Southwestern Louisiana in Lafayette.

1983 He receives a permanent appointment as writer in residence at the University of Southwestern Louisiana; *A Gathering of Old Men* is published.

1993 *A Lesson Before Dying*, Gaines's sixth novel, is nominated for the Pulitzer Prize and wins the National Book Critics Circle Award; Gaines marries Dianne Saulney, a Miami attorney originally from Louisiana, and begins spending part of each year in Miami; he is awarded a MacArthur Fellowship.

2000 Gaines is awarded the National Humanities Medal, the Louisiana Writer Award, the National Governors' Arts Award, membership in the American Academy of Arts and Letters, and is made a Chevalier of France's Order of Arts and Letters.

2005 *Mozart and Leadbelly*, a collection of essays, short stories, and interviews, is published.

2007 The Baton Rouge Area Foundation establishes the Ernest J. Gaines Award to honor the best newly published African-American writers from across the United States.

NOTES

Chapter 1

1 Valerie Melissa Babb, *Ernest Gaines*. Boston: Twayne Publishers, 1991, p. 5.

2 Ibid.

3 Anne K. Simpson, *A Gathering of Gaines: The Man and the Writer*. Lafayette: The Center for Louisiana Studies, University of Southwestern Louisiana, 1991, p. 31.

4 John Lowe, ed., *Conversations with Ernest Gaines*. Jackson: University Press of Mississippi, 1995, p. 86.

5 Karen Carmean, *Ernest J. Gaines: A Critical Companion*. Westport, Conn.: Greenwood Press, 1998, p. 19.

Chapter 2

1 Lowe, *Conversations with Ernest Gaines*, p. 138.

2 Carmean, *Ernest J. Gaines*, p. 2.

3 Carmean, *Ernest J. Gaines*, p. 1.

4 Simpson, *A Gathering of Gaines*, p. 3.

5 Lowe, *Conversations with Ernest Gaines*, pp. 50–51.

6 Simpson, *A Gathering of Gaines*, pp. 6–7.

7 Simpson, *A Gathering of Gaines*, pp. 8–9.

8 Simpson, *A Gathering of Gaines*, p. 10.

9 Simpson, *A Gathering of Gaines*, pp. 12–13.

Chapter 3

1 Carmean, *Ernest J. Gaines*, p. 3.

2 Simpson, *A Gathering of Gaines*, p. 14.

3 Simpson, *A Gathering of Gaines*, p. 15.

4 Ernest J. Gaines, *Mozart and Leadbelly*. New York: Vintage Books, 2005, p. 7.

5 Gaines, *Mozart and Leadbelly*, p. 8.

6 Gaines, *Mozart and Leadbelly*, pp. 8–9.

7 Simpson, *A Gathering of Gaines*, pp. 16–17.

8 Simpson, *A Gathering of Gaines*, p. 17.

9 Carmean, *Ernest J. Gaines*, p. 4.

10 Simpson, *A Gathering of Gaines*, p. 17.

11 Simpson, *A Gathering of Gaines*, p. 18.

12 Simpson, *A Gathering of Gaines*, p. 19.

13 Gaines, *Mozart and Leadbelly*, p. 13.

14 Carmean, *Ernest J. Gaines*, p. 5.

Chapter 4

1 Simpson, *A Gathering of Gaines*, p. 23.

2 Carmean, *Ernest J. Gaines*, p. 6.

3 Marcia Gaudet and Carl Wooton, *Porch Talk with Ernest Gaines: Conversations on the Writer's Craft*. Baton Rouge: Louisiana State University Press, 1990, p. 114.

4 Gaudet and Wooton, *Porch Talk with Ernest Gaines*, p. 115.

5 Simpson, *A Gathering of Gaines*, p. 28.

6 Lowe, *Conversations with Ernest Gaines*, p. 162.

7 Babb, *Ernest Gaines*, p. 6.

8 Lowe, *Conversations with Ernest Gaines*, pp. 7–8.

9 Babb, *Ernest Gaines*, p. 7.

10 Ibid.

11 Lowe, *Conversations with Ernest Gaines*, pp. 35–36.

12 Lowe, *Conversations with Ernest Gaines*, pp. 12–13.

Chapter 5

1 Babb, *Ernest Gaines*, p. 76.

2 Babb, *Ernest Gaines*, p. 79.

3 Ibid.

4 Gaines, *Mozart and Leadbelly*, p. 22.

5 Ibid.

6 Lowe, *Conversations with Ernest Gaines*, p. 103.

7 Ernest J. Gaines, *The Autobiography of Miss Jane Pittman*. New York: Bantam Books, 1972, p. iv.

8 Simpson, *A Gathering of Gaines*, pp. 265–266.

9 Alice Walker. "Review of *The Autobiography of Miss Jane Pittman*." *New York Times*, May 23, 1971. http://select.nytimes.com/mem/archive/pdf?res=F30710F8355F127A93C1AB178ED85F458785F9.

10 Simpson, *A Gathering of Gaines*, p. 266.

11 Lowe, *Conversations with Ernest Gaines*, p. 247.

Chapter 6

1 Lowe, *Conversations with Ernest Gaines*, p. 71.

2 Lowe, *Conversations with Ernest Gaines*, p. 155.

3 Lowe, *Conversations with Ernest Gaines*, p. 248.

4 Lowe, *Conversations with Ernest Gaines*, p. 142.

5 Lowe, *Conversations with Ernest Gaines*, p. 88.

6 Lowe, *Conversations with Ernest Gaines*, pp. 162–163.

7 Carmean, *Ernest J. Gaines*, p. 9.

8 Lowe, *Conversations with Ernest Gaines*, p. 167.

9 Lowe, *Conversations with Ernest Gaines*, p. 243.

10 Lowe, *Conversations with Ernest Gaines*, p. 168.

11 Simpson, *A Gathering of Gaines*, p. 323.

12 Simpson, *A Gathering of Gaines*, p. 324.

13 Ibid.

14 Simpson, *A Gathering of Gaines*, p. 327.

Chapter 7

1 Simpson, *A Gathering of Gaines*, p. 81.

2 Simpson, *A Gathering of Gaines*, pp. 81–82.

3 Lowe, *Conversations with Ernest Gaines*, p. 246.

4 Simpson, *A Gathering of Gaines*, p. 233.

5 Lowe, *Conversations with Ernest Gaines*, p. 247.

6 Lowe, *Conversations with Ernest Gaines*, pp. 197–198.

7 Gaines, *Mozart and Leadbelly*, p. 60.

8 *Chicago Tribune*, "Review of *A Lesson Before Dying*," front cover, *A Lesson Before Dying*, by Ernest J. Gaines. New York: Vintage Books, 1993.

9 Lowe, *Conversations with Ernest Gaines*, p. 281.

10 Ibid.

11 Ibid.

12 Lowe, *Conversations with Ernest Gaines*, p. 296.

Chapter 8

1 Carmean, *Ernest J. Gaines*, p. 11.

2 "About the Fellows Program." The John D. and Catherine T. MacArthur Foundation. http://www.macfound.org/site/c.lkLXJ8MQKrH/b.4536879/k.9B87/About_the_Program.htm.

3 Ibid.

4 Lowe, *Conversations with Ernest Gaines*, p. 326.

5 Lowe, *Conversations with Ernest Gaines*, p. 247.

6 "Home Page." The Ernest J. Gaines Award for Literary Excellence. http://www.ernestgainesaward.org.

7 Erik Spanberg. "Gaines Tells the Stories of His People and His Land." *Christian Science Monitor*, October 4, 2005. http://www.csmonitor.com/2005/1004/p16as01-bogn.html.

8 Lowe, *Conversations with Ernest Gaines*, p. 68.

WORKS BY ERNEST J. GAINES

1964 *Catherine Carmier*

1967 *Of Love and Dust*

1968 *Bloodline*

1971 *The Autobiography of Miss Jane Pittman*

1978 *In My Father's House*

1983 *A Gathering of Old Men*

1993 *A Lesson Before Dying*

2005 *Mozart and Leadbelly*

POPULAR BOOKS

THE AUTOBIOGRAPHY OF MISS JANE PITTMAN

Gaines's best-known book, *The Autobiography of Miss Jane Pittman* is the fictional life story of a 110-year-old African-American woman. Through her life story, readers experience the sweep of black history in the American South, from slavery to sharecropping to the beginnings of the civil rights movement.

BLOODLINE

This collection of five short stories, "A Long Day in November," "The Sky Is Gray," "Three Men," "Bloodline," and "Just Like a Tree," looks at the effects of racism on African-American men at different moments in their lives. The first two stories in the collection have come to be considered masterpieces of the short-story form.

A GATHERING OF OLD MEN

A Cajun boss, Beau Boutan, has been killed in front of the cabin of Mathu, an older African-American man who has spent his life working on the Marshall Plantation. When Sheriff Mapes arrives to investigate the crime, he is confronted with a remarkable scene: Nearly all of the plantation's older black men are there, all armed with recently fired shotguns, swearing that they killed Boutan. Through their stories, the reader learns about life on the plantation, discovers a history of racism both past and present, and observes the "old men" standing up for themselves as men for perhaps the first time in their lives.

A LESSON BEFORE DYING

After a young black man named Jefferson takes part in a shootout in which three men are killed, he is convicted of murder and sentenced to death. Grant Wiggins, who left the plantation's small community for the university, has returned home to teach at the plantation school. His aunt and Jefferson's godmother convince him to visit Jefferson in his prison cell to teach him self-respect, to become a "man" before he is executed. Through their conversations, both men change in unexpected ways and come to realize the heroism that exists in simply resisting and defying the expected.

POPULAR CHARACTERS

GRANT WIGGINS

The narrator and central character of *A Lesson Before Dying*, Wiggins has returned home from college to teach at the plantation school. While trying to teach the condemned prisoner Jefferson how to "be a man," Wiggins is forced to confront his own mixed feelings about returning to the racist society he thought he had been able to escape. Can he be "a man" while living in the South, or will he need to escape and return north to keep his self-respect?

JAMES

The eight-year-old narrator of Gaines's short-story masterpiece "The Sky Is Gray," James travels with his mother from the plantation where they live to the small town of Bayonne to visit the dentist to take care of his toothache. Through their day's journey, James observes the everyday indignities caused by racism but also witnesses acts of kindness and humanity as well.

JANE PITTMAN

The heroine of the fictional autobiography *The Autobiography of Miss Jane Pittman*, Miss Jane is an uneducated yet extraordinary African-American woman whose life span extends from slavery to the beginnings of the civil rights movement.

THE OLD MEN

Not one character but several, "the old men" are at the center of Gaines's 1983 novel, *A Gathering of Old Men*. Through their confrontation with Sheriff Mapes and their confession to a crime that none of them committed, the reader gets a memorable look at racism and the price paid by both the oppressed and the oppressors.

MAJOR AWARDS

1967–1968 Gaines receives a National Endowment for the Arts Study Award.

1972 He receives a Guggenheim Fellowship, the California Commonwealth Gold Medal Award for *The Autobiography of Miss Jane Pittman*, and the Louisiana Literary Award for *The Autobiography of Miss Jane Pittman*.

1993 He wins the Dos Passos Prize and is named a John D. and Catherine T. MacArthur Foundation fellow; *A Lesson Before Dying* earns the National Book Critics Circle Award.

2000 Gaines wins numerous awards, including the National Humanities Medal, the Louisiana Writer Award, and the National Governors' Arts Award. He is elected a member in the American Academy of Arts and Letters Department of Literature and is made a Chevalier of France's Order of Arts and Letters.

BIBLIOGRAPHY

Books

Babb, Valerie Melissa. *Ernest Gaines*. Boston: Twayne Publishers, 1991.

Carmean, Karen. *Ernest J. Gaines: A Critical Companion*. Westport, Conn.: Greenwood Press, 1998.

Eshelman-Lee, Julie. *Antoine Decuir and His Legacy: River Lake Plantation*. Fort Collins, Colo.: Creole West Productions, 2003.

Gaines, Ernest J. *The Autobiography of Miss Jane Pittman*. New York: Bantam Books, 1972.

———. *Bloodline*: *Five Stories*. New York: Vintage Books, 1997.

———. *Catherine Carmier*. New York: Vintage Books, 1994.

———. *A Gathering of Old Men*. New York: Vintage Books, 1992.

———. *A Lesson Before Dying*. New York: Vintage Books, 1993.

———. *Mozart and Leadbelly*. New York: Vintage Books, 2005.

Gaudet, Marcia, and Carl Wooton. *Porch Talk with Ernest Gaines: Conversations on the Writer's Craft*. Baton Rouge: Louisiana State University Press, 1990.

Lowe, John, ed. *Conversations with Ernest Gaines*. Jackson: University Press of Mississippi, 1995.

Simpson, Anne K. *A Gathering of Gaines: The Man and the Writer*. Lafayette: The Center for Louisiana Studies, University of Southwestern Louisiana, 1991.

Web Sites

"Biography of Ernest Gaines," Academy of Achievement. Available online. URL: http://www.achievement.org/autodoc/page/gaiobio-1.

Bryerman, Keith E. "Biography of Ernest Gaines," Dictionary of Literary Biography. Available online. URL: http://www.bookrags.com/biography/ernest-james-gaines-dlb3.

Ferris, Bill. "Meeting Ernest Gaines: A Conversation with Ernest Gaines," *Humanities*, July/August 1998. Available online. URL: http://www.neh.gov/news/humanities/1998-07/gaines-html.

"Home for Good: Author's Work Will Be Preserved in New Center in Dupre Library," *La Louisiane*, Spring 2008. Available online. URL: http://www.louisiana.edu/Advancement/PRNS/lala/2008-Spring/gainescenter.pdf.

Spanberg, Erik. "Gaines Tells the Stories of His People and His Land," *Christian Science Monitor*, October 4, 2005. Available online. URL: http://www.csmonitor.com/2005/1004/p16s01-bogn.html.

The Ernest J. Gaines Award for Literary Excellence. Available online. URL: http://www.ernestgainesaward.org.

The John D. and Catherine T. MacArthur Foundation. Available online. URL: http://www.macfound.org.

Walker, Alice. "Review of *The Autobiography of Miss Jane Pittman*," *New York Times*, May 23, 1971. Available online. URL: http://select.nytimes.com/mem/archive/pdf?res=F30710F8355F127A93C1AB178ED85F458785F9.

FURTHER READING

Books

Botkin, B.A., ed. *Lay My Burden Down: A Folk History of Slavery*. New York: Delta, 1973.

Cather, Willa. *My Antonia*. New York: Simon and Schuster, 2004.

Gaines, Ernest. Foreword to *Wide Awake in the Pelican State: Stories by Contemporary Louisiana Writers*, edited by Ann Brewster Dobie. Baton Rouge: Louisiana State University Press, 2006.

Turgenev, Ivan. *Fathers and Sons*. New York: Signet Classics, 2005.

———. *Sketches from a Hunter's Album: The Complete Edition*. New York: Penguin Classics, 1990.

Welty, Eudora. *The Collected Stories of Eudora Welty*. New York: Harvest Books, 1982.

PICTURE CREDITS

page:

10: Andrew McKinney/© photolibrary. All rights reserved

14: AP Images

17: © Philip Gould/CORBIS

20: akg-images

24: © Philip Gould/CORBIS

32: Hulton Archive/Getty Images

46: Newhouse News Service/Landov

54: Michael Ochs Archives/Getty Images

60: CBS Photo Archive/Hulton Archive/Getty Images

68: AP Images

75: BIOSCOP/ZENITH/CONSOLIDATED/THE KOBAL COLLECTION

80: © Gerrit de Heus/Alamy

83: AP Images

92: © Sophie Bassouls/Sygma/Corbis

INDEX

ABOUT THE CONTRIBUTOR

DENNIS ABRAMS is the author of several books for Chelsea House, including biographies of Barbara Park, Hamid Karzai, Albert Pujols, Xerxes, Rachael Ray, and Hillary Rodham Clinton. He attended Antioch College, where he majored in English and communications. A voracious reader since the age of three, Dennis lives in Houston, Texas, with his partner of 21 years, along with their two cats and their dog, Junie B.